Bring In Donuts

And 35 other sweet tips to transform your career today.

by Darcy Miller, J.D.

Copyright © 2018 by Darcy Miller

All rights reserved. No part of this publication may be reproduced, stored, or transmitted in any form or by any means, electronic, mechanical, photocopying, recording, scanning, or otherwise, except as permitted under Section 107 or 108 of the 1976 United States Copyright Act, without the prior written permission of the author.

Limitation of liability/disclaimer of warranty: While the publisher and author have used their best efforts in preparing book, they make no representations or warranties with respect to the accuracy or completeness of the contents and specifically disclaim any implied warranties of merchantability or fitness for particular purpose.

The advice and strategies contained herein may not be suitable for your situation. You should consult with a professional where appropriate. Neither the publisher nor author shall be liable for any loss of profit or any other commercial damages, including but not limited to special, incidental, consequential, or other damages.

Book cover designed by Allison McAuley.
Illustrations drawn by Anna Lena van Iersel.

Names: Miller, Darcy, 1977- author.
Title: Bring in donuts : and 35 other sweet tips to transform your career today / Darcy Miller, J.D.
Description: Auburn Hills, MI : Pivotal Publishers, 2018.
Identifiers: ISBN 978-1-7323235-0-6 (pbk.) | ISBN 978-1-7323235-1-3 (ebook)
Subjects: LCSH: Career development. | Success in business. | Success--Psychological aspects. | Quality of work life. | Motivation (Psychology) | Self-actualization. | BISAC: SELF-HELP / Personal Growth / Success. | BUSINESS & ECONOMICS / Personal Success. | BUSINESS & ECONOMICS / Workplace Culture.
Classification: LCC BF637.S8 M56 2018 (print) | LCC BF637.S8 (ebook) | DDC 158.26--dc23.

Dedication

To my sweet kiddos: Zander, Jacey and Nash. Life is indescribably better because of each of you. I'm so immensely proud to be your mom. Thanks for bringing me so much joy and loving me unconditionally every single day.

To my love: Todd. Thank you for picking me. Thank you for believing in me to pursue my crazy dreams. Thank you for making the kid's lunches. You are the unsung hero in our family. I love you this much.

Praise for Bring in Donuts

"Bring in Donuts should be required reading for anyone who works for a living. Darcy's advice is like that of a trusted friend/mentor, offering a variety of practical methods to increase effectiveness. Darcy's authenticity and humor shines through on every page. Buy this book - and then buy some donuts."
– *Chris Olt Nieuwsma, Vice President Human Resources*

"Bring in Donuts takes the "bite" out of navigating your career. With its insightful, hilarious and refreshing tips; this books makes it easy to transform your career. "
– *Mimi Brown, Leadership Expert and President, AMP Up Success*

"This book is perfect for anyone who wants to be reminded (or in some cases told for the first time) of the simple, practical and yet so often overlooked fundamental principles of workplace interaction. Just don't read it if you're hungry!"
– *John R. Clark, President, Corporate Counsel Solutions PLC*

"I had the pleasure of working with the author at a large advertising agency where, in hindsight most of or co-workers probably would have benefitted tremendously from reading it. Bring in Donuts reflects what I recall about working with Darcy: smart, funny, does not take itself too seriously and incredibly original."
– *Mike Pardi*

Contents

Introduction 1

Connect *You can't build a career by yourself. No matter how amazing you are in the workplace.* 3

    Bring in Donuts: Breaking Bread Together 3
    Be Present 6
    Ask Questions 10
    Listen Well 13
    Find Common Ground 16
    Refrain from Judgment 20
    Be Humble (Don't One-Up Them) 22
    Share Failures / Be Relatable. 25
    Be Kind 27
    Real Life Example 30

Communicate *How to communicate in a clear, concise and actionable way. Every single day.* 33

    Be Honest. 35
    Be Respectful. 38
    Ask the Right Questions. 41
    Be Clear and Concise. 46
    Provide The Right Amount of Information 49
    Know Your Audience 51

Follow-up/Finish 54

Practical Tips 56

Real life Examples 66

Collaborate *How to play well with your colleagues - and still get the job done.* 69

Be Prepared 70

Anticipate Questions/Bring Solutions 73

Be Resourceful 76

Work Hard 79

Be Accountable/Expect Accountability 81

Be Coachable 84

Lead By Example 87

Make Your Boss's Job Easier 89

Real-Life Example 92

Have Fun *You spend too much time at the workplace not to have some fun once in a while.* 95

Laugh Together 96

Decorate 98

Monthly Events 101

Activities 104

Start a Club 106

Donate 108

Learn Something 110

Real Life Example 112

Gratitude *Showing gratitude in the workplace will truly set you apart from all of your colleagues. And it feels pretty incredible.* 113

    Say Thank You. 114

    Type Thank You. 116

    Write Thank You. 118

    Bonus: Traveling Gratitude Board 120

    Real Life Example 121

Conclusion *Go find your local donut shop. This morning.* 123

Preface

This book was never part of the plan. The plan was always to read everyone else's books – and to be a consumer of other people's thoughts and ideas with a pen and highlighter in hand.

Yet, over a period of several years, dozens and dozens of people asked for my advice on how to successfully navigate the workplace because of the way I conducted myself at work. While I was helping them on their professional journey, it turns out they were helping me in a bigger way. They helped me to genuinely believe that these tips and skills could make a difference – in a career, in an organization and in the world.

After some nudging from a variety of people, it was time to start writing a book that showcases the actionable and fun tips that have helped me and so many others find easy ways to transform our careers.

So, here it is...the book that was never part of the plan. Hopefully this book will make you smile, while making your career a bit more successful. Enjoy!

Acknowledgements

Writing a book takes a village. Self-publishing a book takes an even bigger village. Here's a small start of my gratitude:

Mom and Dad – Thanks for instilling such incredible values in me at such a young age and for never clipping my wings. You have always let me fly!

Korin – Thanks for being my best friend and the perfect brainstorming partner.

Regina – Thanks for coaching me and encouraging me to take this journey.

Blast from the Cast – Regina, Verick, Lem, Allie, Bethany and Robin. Thanks for inspiring me to chase my dreams.

Laurie – Thanks for helping me to keep my health a priority, despite the self-inflicted stress of writing a book.

Tonya – Thanks for being a guiding light and for reminding me that I'm so much more than just a lawyer.

Mimi – Thanks for being my cheerleader and such a resourceful friend during this entire process.

Alli – Thanks for designing such a gorgeous book cover.

Friends – Thanks to each of you who have endlessly supported me and helped make this book a reality.

Colleagues – Thanks to everyone I've ever worked with over the years. You are all woven into my professional career – and I'm better because of each of you.

Todd – Thank you for loving me, supporting me and being my rock.

Book launch team – Adrienne Mueller, Allie Smith, Allison McAuley, Amanda Aude, Angela Parker, Ann-Marie Transki, Bailey Stephens, Barbara Marsman, Becky Cox, Bethany Smith, Betsy Deeds, Brad Cox, Brett Cox, Caitlin Moore, Candice Hukka, Cari Clark, Carol Cox, Carrie Duvall, Chris Parker, Christie Dunbar, Christina Contreras, Courtney Zifkin, Dane Fortney, Dawn Gee, Elizabeth Alore, Elizabeth Wyderko, Elizabeth Smith, Fred Chapman, Gayle Hargrave-Thomas, Gloria Wilson, Heather Grattan, Jane Jeannero, Jen Smith, Jenn Friedman, Jessica Berry, Jessica Weiss, Julie Woolley, Kathryn Halteman, Kelli Johnston, Kelly Wooters, Kim Daniels, Korin Visocchi, Kristin Dubuque, Laurie Moro, Lemuel Anaejionu, Lindsey Poprocki, Lisa Thomas, Lisa Avery, Lori Zancourides, Luke Marsman, Marie Chapman, Marissa Friese, Mary Lobbestael, Melissa Destross, Melissa Wilhelm, Mónica Ramírez, Natalie Jackson, Pam Purnell, Regina Anaejionu, Robin Walthour, Sally Burns, Samantha Reichbach, Sonia Sobolic, Stacy Hollfelder, Stacy Osborne, Stephanie Rothfuss, Stepheni Vroman, Steven Pitsillos, Susan Canning, Susan Hartung, Todd Miller, Verick Wayne, Veronique Tu and Whitney Cuson.

Thanks for helping to spread the message of this book!!

Introduction

Donuts.

Donuts are the reason some people are more successful than others. Okay, maybe not entirely. (But quite possibly.) I mean, a sugary delight baked in the oven...delish. In reality, donuts are just one of the simple, effective and fun things that we can do to sustain a long, respected and successful career. But why?

Donuts *connect* people. And connecting with others is a crucial part of the foundation of a successful career. Have you ever wondered why some people are more successful than others? Why some people are getting ahead in the workplace, while others seem to be invisible? The answer to that is simpler than it seems. Successful people complete small things every day that add up to the sum of a wonderful career:

They connect.
They communicate.
They collaborate.
They have fun.
They are grateful.

It all starts with you. You can launch your own successful career. You can do it today.

Whether you are on day 1 or day 4,367 of your career, these tips can be implemented as soon as you get back to your desk.

In the pages ahead, you will find tools to boost your career in the right direction, along with real life examples of how to apply these tools. These tools are things you can showcase while you are completing the daily tasks your job, but aren't quite getting to that higher level. You *are capable* of getting to the next level - you just need to learn (or re-learn) some of the soft skills you may not have learned in school.

Think of this book as a crash course in those soft skills. Consider those soft skills as a way to help increase influence, get noticed for all the right things, boost visibility, enhance your perceived value within your workplace and achieve the career you deserve!

Grab that donut, snag a napkin and enjoy!

Connect

You can't build a career by yourself. No matter how amazing you are in the workplace.

Bring in Donuts: Breaking Bread Together

Donuts connect people. Wait...wasn't that already mentioned? Yes. But it bears repeating.

But how do those yummy, sweet, round delights[1] connect you with your colleagues?

It's simple. Food brings people together. It's why most holiday parties have delectable delights, funerals have luncheons with mayo-laden casseroles and most first dates involve stressing over what to pick off the menu (do I order a salad or the burger and/or the decadent dessert?). It connects us – both in the good times and the tough times.

Food helps us relate to others. Some people relate to others when discussing the different diets or eating regimes they are currently on or have done for a lifetime. Some people discuss the food they eat during celebrations, which can lead to discussions about what things they like to celebrate, which can create a deeper relationship.

<u>Food connects us, despite differing levels of sophistication</u>

---
[1] Please know that if you want them to be vegan, low fat or low carb donuts that is cool, too.

in our individual palettes. Personally, my palette is about as basic as they come. However, some of my colleagues like avocados or sushi - which puts them in a different, slightly more elevated hemisphere when it comes to how fancy they are in my book. But talking – and giggling – about what we each like and dislike continues to connect us.

Food creates relationships that might not otherwise exist. How often would you stop at the desk of an unknown colleague to talk about the weather or sports? Probably rarely. But those same unknown colleagues can become cool, unexpected friends at work – because you see them every third morning at the water cooler or at the coffee area. These connections often only originate because of food.

Connecting over food at the workplace can help boost productivity through the established relationships built over a single donut or a dozen donuts in the past year. Companies with brilliantly smart people already know this because they have built cafeterias, food stations and other eateries into their buildings. Productivity can increase when you interact with people from different departments because colleagues are, even if just casually, gaining deeper insights into other areas of the business. These insights can help individuals perform their responsibilities more effectively and can help the bottom line of their employer. People are also more productive when they are surrounded by people who they have a relationship with already – even if the relationship simply stems from a conversation about what type of food they bring with them on camping trips.

Many of us don't save lives for a living. But for those who do, it often takes a well-orchestrated team of people that implements a seamless procedure to save each and every life. Let's take firefighters for example. They literally run into burning buildings as a team. And guess what? They break bread together at the firehouse. They cook together in a community kitchen and eat together as a family. These simple acts connect them and help them to build a cohesive and deep-seeded team that they can rely on in the most dire situations.

Whether you are standing in the work kitchen chatting with a colleague about if you should take half or a whole donut at the office – or having the monthly team lunch meeting – you are breaking bread together and creating/building that connection.

It's easy to find appropriate opportunities to break bread together with colleagues. Grab breakfast before work with your boss on a monthly basis. Bring bagels to the next early morning meeting. Invite your hilarious colleague to lunch every quarter. Be the hero with fresh baked cookies at the next late afternoon meeting. Organize a potluck for the next unconventional holiday. You might just connect with someone who will change the trajectory of your career. Or even better, you might be able to connect with someone over a chocolate donut....and *you* will be able to change the trajectory of their career. Wouldn't that be something?

Bring in donuts. Seriously. People will love you. At least I would love you.

Donuts can change the world.

Be Present

Okay, okay. I know, I know. This little section might seem like a bit of a lecture. It's not meant to be. But it's so important for your career - both today and in the future. So, let's make this section like a popular brand of elastic bandage[2] that you have to rip off very quickly.

Be present.
Make eye contact.
Give your attention.
Sit up straight.
Stop the distractions.
Use their name.
Smile a bit.

You know the drill. Being present can mean several things. It can mean being physically present (rather than checking your phone constantly for new notifications), emotionally present (instead of thinking about something else entirely, despite looking the other person in the eye) or even being prepared for a meeting (did you read the emails/documents that pertain to this meeting?).

But why can't I bury my head in my phone or type an email while talking on the phone or avert my eyes when I see someone walk by? Everyone else is doing it, including the leaders of my company, so why can't I?

Because I said so. [3]

---

[2] Quick little side note. I was an advertising attorney for about 10 years. Part of that job was to protect trademarks and to prevent others from infringing on trademarks. So, as much as I want to use the word that rhymes with Cland-Fade here, I just can't do it. Thanks for understanding the level of my nerdiness.

[3] Just because I said to do this does not mean I'm perfect at this stuff

That would've been a great way to end this section, but let me give you some actual reasons why you should be different than everyone else in this area:

Wasted time. If you aren't present in the conversation/meeting, you are wasting people's valuable time. People are taking time out of their day to work with you on something. If you aren't truly present, then that person should use their time on something else more productive. If you *are* truly present, you can drastically reduce the amount of time you spend working on the project, because you are laser-focused and not distracted. Give people the gift of time. It is a better gift than a donut (gasp!).

Productivity. If you aren't present in the conversation/meeting, you are reducing your own productivity and possibly the productivity of your colleague. You might have missed a few *crucial* pieces of information when you are checking to see what the latest notification was on your phone. That crucial piece of information might be the difference between you nailing that next project or barely squeaking by on it. It might even be the difference between life and death, if you work in the medical field.

Respect. If you aren't present in the conversation/meeting, you are changing (or further cementing) the way you are perceived at work. If you aren't present in the conversation/meeting, it can be simply offensive. We are all busy in our lives. Each of us has an endless to-do list, but some people still remain

---

either. I promise I'm not...but I also promise that when I'm present on a regular basis, more opportunities are presented to me that can help change my career for the better.

respectful enough to be present. If colleagues realize you aren't present, they will find work-arounds rather than work directly with you. You will earn a reputation at work. You just will. Your reputation of not paying attention will precede you. It may even haunt you for quite some time.

Trust. Ouch, this one feels like someone punched you in the gut. If you aren't present in the conversation/meeting, you will lose your trustworthiness. People can't trust you if you only listened to three-quarters or one-third of the conversation. Let that sink in. *People cannot trust you if you aren't present in the conversation.*

Do you ever wonder why you are being passed up for promotions or raises or other accolades at work? It might help to look up from your phone and see what's going on around you.

Stand out. Be a trailblazer. Pay attention during in-person conversations, in meetings and on phone calls.

The good news: You can change all of this today. Today, my friends! Here are two easy ways to be more present:

1. Start by turning off the notifications on your phone. The messages will still be there when you are ready to work on them.

2. Think to yourself, *would I treat my grandma this way? By not being present with her?* No way.

Those two tips alone will allow you to be more present during every interaction and you will see what it does for you and your career!

BRING IN DONUTS

Now, was that too harsh? Hopefully it was simply insightful and not harsh. But seriously, I would rather see your eyes than your forehead...

Your presence isn't what's needed, it's being present that is what's needed.

Ask Questions

One of the super-duper secrets of developing meaningful relationships with others (including loved ones and colleagues) is so simple: Ask questions.

Once you are in a conversation with someone who you are connecting with and the other person knows that you are fully present with them, engage with them. Find out more about them. One of the best ways to truly learn more about someone is to ask them insightful questions. Learn about what makes them happy. Learn about what makes them concerned. These organic conversations will help deepen any connection.

When people answer these questions, it means they trust you. And as previously mentioned, trust is the foundation of any connection. What a compliment to you that they trust you so much!

The insights gained from these conversations will also be valuable in any future interactions with them. It's like having an ethical and easy cheat sheet on how to successfully work with one of your colleagues, because now you know what makes them tick.

While most people love to chat about themselves, often they don't share some of the most valuable nuggets about themselves. That's where the fun, simple, not-creepy questions come into place. When there is a natural break in their talking, ask a question either related to what they just said or share something slightly personal about yourself, followed up by a related question.

A quick warning, my friends: Please don't use this section

as a green light to *interrogate* someone. Peppering someone with questions will do the opposite of connecting with them, it will scare/annoy/make their skin crawl. Also, please don't sound like a robot. Rather, ask questions in an easy going way.

Here are some of my absolute favorite questions to ask during a casual conversation:

"What's your favorite kind of donut?" (Obviously.) [Use this in any context...especially if you are near a place that houses food. Of course, if you don't care about donuts (which is statistically highly unlikely), replace with any other food/drink.]

"Jimmy, any big plans for the evening/weekend/break?" [This is great for Fridays or right before a holiday break, when people maybe aren't as productive and are looking for a way to spend a few less minutes getting back to their work. Also, you may find out something simply fascinating about them...maybe they are a lead singer in a local band or run marathons or have an art booth at art fairs.]

"Jamie, what did you do over the weekend/break?" [Perfect for Monday mornings or the first day back after break, when people are easing back into their workload. Again, you may find out something simply fascinating about them...maybe they went to the same college as you or take amazing photos or cheer for the same favorite sports team.]

"Jimmy, have you tried any new recipes lately?" [What a great question if you are discussing or are around food. You can connect with them if (a) you both h*te to cook; (b) you both love to cook; or (c) you have polar opposite opinions about how you like your steak prepared, but can

get a good laugh about it anyways.]

"Jamie, have you seen any good movies lately?" [Classic. For any situation.]

"Jimmy, can you recommend any good binge-worthy shows?" [Timely and relevant question. Imagine all the possibilities you can connect with someone on this question. You might find the only other person in the office who loves cooking shows as much as you (and you can exchange favorite recipes), or horror shoes, or sci-fi shows. This one gets right down into the soul of someone. Ask away!]

"How about those Detroit Lions?" [This is a very specific question for a very specific region for a very brave soul. Use this question wisely.]

Asking insightful questions will set you apart from everyone at the workplace.

Listen Well

Alright, my friends. We have connected over some food, remained present with them and have asked some incredibly insightful questions. Are you done yet? Nope! Now we *actively* listen to them and take an interest into what they are saying. This skill takes a connection from a decent/casual connection to a trusted colleague in the workplace.

So, how do we listen well?

Look them in the eyes. Eye contact is one of the most powerful ways to connect with someone. It proves to them that they have their attention.

Put away your phone. Even if you just put the phone face down, it gives the signal that you are ready to participate in the conversation.

***Slightly* nod your head.** Again, let's avoid appearing robotic...natural, subtle head nods here.

Smile. Show them your pearly whites! Smiling can ease an awkward conversation and lead to even more smiling.

Uncross your arms. This body language just screams anger or unhappiness. We don't want to be angry or unhappy when we are connecting with someone.

Give them regular feedback. This could be an audible, "hmm, hmmm" or "Oh my word!" (a personal favorite) or "That sounds like an awful situation." This confirms that you are listening to their story and not day-dreaming about what snack you brought for the afternoon.

Say their name. Yes, it's that simple. Say their name out loud. Just think about when someone that you don't know that well actually says your name. It means that you matter to that person. That's powerful stuff.

No interrupting. Refrain from interrupting them or looking like you are going to interrupt them. They are probably responding to your question, so give them the time and respect to answer accordingly. Interrupting or finishing their sentences can simply derail a perfectly lovely conversation because the listener is following their own thoughts, instead of listening to what the speaker is saying. Interrupting makes it seem like the other person thinks they have something more important to say or that they don't really care what the other person thinks. Avoid pointing at them or opening your mouth as they are still elaborating their statement. If someone looks like they are just chomping at the bit to respond, it often means they are no longer listening - and instead are just waiting to talk. Know the difference - and please just keep listening.

Actively listening is a *gift* to both people. It is a gift to the person listening, because the speaker trusts (see the theme of trust in this little book) the listener with some of their personal information and wants to spend some of their time with the listener as well. It is a gift to the person sharing their story, because it shows that the listener values the speaker; the listener thinks the speaker is important and respects them enough to take time out of their (presumably) busy day to chat with them.

By listening with purpose, you are single-handedly making them feel like the most important person on earth. Honestly, how many people in your daily encounters make you feel that way? At home, everyone is just getting trying to get the chores done. At work, everyone is just trying to get the projects done. Most people seem overwhelmed in their lives and barely give their favorite people in the world their undivided attention. Imagine how much you would stand out if you made people feel this important at the workplace? Just imagine it.

Actively listening is just that, an action. It isn't a passive thing. It takes practice and it takes time to craft the skill. It is a skill that is worth mastering as soon as possible in your career because it not only makes you stand out, but it fosters a stronger work environment. So get to active and purposeful listening, my friends!

Please remember that listening does not obligate you to agree with them. It just extends your respect to them, while connecting with them at the same time.

One last tip: Let's turn the tables for a moment. Who do you enjoy talking with? Why? How do they make you feel? Important? Understood? Whatever they actively do when you converse with them, take a mental note and use those same techniques during the next conversation you have with someone. You can make someone else feel as amazing as they make you feel.

Actively listening will get you farther in life than actively talking.

Find Common Ground

Excellent work, my friends. Our colleagues recognize how fun and trustworthy you are, as they have shared some of their life's journey with you (whether very casually or very intensely).

Now comes the fun part. Let's figure out what you have in common with them! Finding common ground is a way to genuinely bond with them. For most of you, this comes very naturally (and you might even be able to skip this section), but for others, this is a foreign concept and it can seem a bit overwhelming when you don't know what to say.

Since you are already asking insightful questions AND listening actively to what they are saying in response to your amazing questions, you will have lots of material to use as a basis to find similarities. Once you discover that you have common ground, mention it to them with enthusiasm!

Sports. This is such a great way to further deepen a connection. Avid sports fans are not quiet about it, so this should be one of the easiest ways to find a common ground with someone. Often, they talk about their teams, wear shirts with their team's logo, showcase logos on their vehicles or have foam fingers from each team (or is that just me?).

Here are some examples...not necessarily something that you need to copy verbatim in a conversation. These are simply concepts to use as part of a casual and organic interaction between people talking about common interests.

BRING IN DONUTS

"Wow - I love/hate the _____ (insert favorite team), too! When was the last time you were at a game?"

"Can you believe _____ (insert any recent, outrageous play/outcome)?"

"Those _____ (insert favorite team with a hint of sarcasm)."

Alumni. Another easy way to find a similarity with a colleague is if you went to the same high school, college or university. Even if you never went to their school, you may still be passionate or knowledgeable about their school. Similar to sports, avid alumni are not hard to find. Check out the walls of their office...do they have diplomas from their alma mater? Have you checked out their LinkedIn profile? Does it show where they went to school?

"How cool! I went to _____ University/College, as well. Have you been back to campus lately?"

"How cool! My son/daughter goes to _____ University/College, as well. My entire paycheck is paying for the new dorms (if you are feeling light-hearted). Glad to see such a great success story (meaning the other person) come out of _____ University/College."

Hobbies/Interests. Based on the example questions in this section, any answers they give you that you can relate with are solid gold in terms of finding common ground. Don't just internally think that you also like/dislike that hobby/interest, tell them out loud.

"Oh my word! _____ (movie/book) was incredible! The _____ (characters/plot/casting) was terrific. Have you read/seen the sequel?"

Jobs/Companies. Sometimes you may have had the same job as the other person or worked at the same company as the other person. This can be quite personal, which will lead to an in-depth and productive connection with them.

"Hey – I worked at _____ (previous company), too! What a small world! What department were you in? Did you know _____ (name of someone well-respected in the company)? _____ (name of company) had great _____ (name something light-hearted and pleasant about the company: coffee, holiday parties, seminars, parking situations, etc.) Do you still keep in touch with anyone from there?"

Same Boss. This similarity can be incredibly useful in the workplace, however, proceed with caution. Please don't use this common ground as a way to bash or criticize that same boss/leader. Use it as a constructive piece of information that can help you, your newly connected colleague and/or your boss.

"How long have you been working with _____ (insert name of boss)? They have been terrific when they _____ (insert something you respect/like about them – this alerts them that you are not interested in gossip or bad-mouthing your respective boss).

One word of caution: While you are conjuring these similarities, make sure that you don't come on too strong. If they aren't actively participating in the conversation, then you can certainly connect with them about these things at a later, more opportune time. If you see more of the side of their face (since they are stretching their neck to see who else they can chat with or looking at the wall clock), then rein it in a bit. Again, this isn't an interrogation...it's a casual connecting of colleagues. (Say that 10 times fast!)

That being said, here's are some of the great things about finding common ground with a colleague:

- You might end up with a small inside joke together – which makes the days so much more enjoyable.
- You might be able to better relate to certain work situations in the future – which might help you excel during a difficult project.
- You might be able to help them in a personal or professional situation in the future.
- You might be able to get them tickets to their favorite sports team.
- Best of all – you might just have more fun at work!!

Working through tough situations is easier if you have already established some similarities.

Refrain from Judgment

I genuinely wish this topic didn't have to be in this book. But, alas, it deserves a few moments of our time.

Similar to being present during conversations, refraining from judgment is another crucially important, yet challenging part of connecting with others.

Now that we have more details about other people's lives, including some possibly personal information...it is imperative that we don't judge them on it – whether silently or gossiping about it with another person. *Imperative.*

Let's remember that everyone has something that keeps us up at night. No one is exempt from sadness, embarrassment, struggle or despair. While our colleagues are sharing some stories with you that might make you instinctively judge them or judge their decisions, *please* don't do it.

Please don't judge them on their style, or their parenting choices, or their favorite sports team or any of the other offensive ways we might be quick to judge someone.

We all have our own unique journeys. The stress and devastation that might be quietly haunting your colleague is omitted from the stories they are sharing with you. Things that could be impacting your colleagues or their family are: divorce, financial problems, tough medical diagnoses, custody battles, addiction, depression, behavioral issues of children, parents with dementia, house fire – and the list goes on and on. More often than not, you won't know about those devastating situations and you

BRING IN DONUTS

won't know their entire journey within the first three conversations you've had with them over donuts in the cafeteria.

We don't know what is keeping them up at night, so give them a bit of grace when you are connecting with them. You will certainly need some grace and kindness, when (not if) one of those horrific situations comes across your journey.

Unless you are an officer of the court who has been elected or nominated to be a judge or magistrate, please refrain from judging others.

Whew - another difficult section out of the way!

Leave the judging to the judges.

Be Humble (Don't One-Up Them)

Humility is the unsung hero of most people's career success stories. Humility isn't loud, bold or super exciting. It's not the coolest kid in the cafeteria. It is often unnoticed and confused with weakness.

Humility is *actually* the sign of someone who is inclusive, gracious, curious, confident, attentive, courteous and strong. Humility lets other people participate in conversations and come together as a team to make big changes. Humble people are well-liked and respected in the office. Colleagues love to work with humble colleagues and supervisors enjoy managing humble workers. Aren't those the types of leaders we want to work for - and eventually want to be?!

In practical circumstances, humility is more of an art than science, that much is true. Too little humility = a j*rk. Too much humility = not confident and passed over for opportunities (because they don't know how amazing you are).

Humility is a powerful skill that can become part of our career success equation.

Connecting at the workplace and relating to others by sharing a similar story or situation is a tried and true way to deepen connections. However, this is where the art of humility comes in... we need to make sure that we don't *accidentally* one-up them.

Examples of *accidentally* one-upping them:

"Wow! You've been to thirty-six states. That's such a big deal! I've been to all fifty. And I wrote a bestselling book about it."

"Congrats on becoming a VP this week. Isn't it great being a VP?...I was the youngest VP in our company's history."

"Neat. You are making all of your kid's food from organic food? We love making our food, too! I have a functioning farm in my suburban backyard where I make all of my food from scratch."

Do these conversations ring a bell? Ding, ding. They are terribly uncomfortable. What are we supposed to say in response to those one-ups? Instead of one-upping them, try these other approaches to better relate (and remain humble, yet powerful and articulate):

"Wow! You've been to 36 states. Isn't traveling around the US such a _____ (humble/terrific/etc.) experience? We've had the opportunity to travel around the US as well. Which state was your favorite?" (Most likely, the other person will answer and then ask you a similar question - and thus, a true connection is made!)

"Congrats on becoming a VP this week. Becoming part of leadership is such an honor and something to be proud of at _____ (name of company). We are so happy you are a rising leader here. If you ever need anything, please let me know." (Ta da! You have remained humble and helpful at the same time. You are connecting and mentoring as a bonus – without sounding too arrogant. Nice work!)

"Neat. You are making all of your kid's food from organic food? That is such an amazing gift to your kids. We were happy to make our kid's food as well when they were little. What foods do your kids like best?" (Bingo! You've remained relatable without one-upping them to make their accomplishments feel less important than your accomplishments. Love it!)

How cool are those conversational techniques to remain engaged, yet humble?!

Let's remember: Humility *does not* mean that we are not proud of our accomplishments, nor does it make us a passive doormat. It *does* mean to be proud of those accomplishments – and to communicate them in just the right dosage.

Lead with humility! Lead with humility!

Humility is the unsung hero of most successful careers.

Share Failures / Be Relatable

Look how far we've come in connecting with our colleagues!! We are connecting on a personal level, finding common ground, refraining from judgment and remaining humble. Are we done with this whole connecting thing yet? Not quite, my friend. Not quite.

Let's consider this section as a bonus tip! This tip will set you apart from the crowd in a good way.

Failures. Ugh. Just typing it can make a person's skin crawl (like mine). Now there are entire incredible books on how great it is to turn failures into monumental learning lessons. Those books will inevitably mention Thomas Edison and how he viewed his 10,000 failures as 10,000 learning opportunities. Side note: That man is probably the most patient man that ever lived. 10,000 failures?! After failing six times at something, I'm ready to throw in the towel. I digress. This section has nothing to do with that timeless adage of Thomas Edison's 10,000 failures.

Instead, let's talk about how sharing some of our funny/relatable failures can be one of the steps in strengthening a great connection at the workplace.

[Someone has just tripped in front of you.] "Jimmy, are you okay? (Assuming he is okay, then continue...if not, then get help for poor Jimmy!) That carpet can sneak up and grab your shoe, can't it? I've tripped here more than once...including once in front of an executive."

[Someone has just burned some popcorn in the kitchen at work.] "Jamie, that s*cks. Don't worry, it's no big deal.

Are you able to salvage the popcorn or get new popcorn? Burned popcorn is the worst. During the first week of my first job, I blew up the microwave with a bag of popcorn. Flames were coming out of the microwave and it stained the wall."

[Someone hurt themselves while playing a recreation sport outside of work hours and have returned to work on crutches.] "Jimmy, oh my word! How are you feeling? How long will you be on crutches? Isn't being on crutches the worst? When I was 16 years old, I was so excited about driver's training that I jumped up to touch the ceiling and then twisted my ankle on the way down and was on crutches the entire summer."

When you know that someone else has made the same mistake, doesn't it make you feel a bit better? That you aren't alone? That even amazing people make mistakes? So, give yourself permission to share the small, kind of silly failures without one-upping them. Then build up your immunity to share even more relatable failures in the appropriate context. It makes you more approachable and the other person will feel less embarrassed about their failures. Win-win!!

As you rise the ladder into leadership in your industry, this skill of sharing failures truly will help you and the people you lead. It will help cultivate people who have the confidence and approval to try things outside of the box.

Failures are like little growing pains that eventually make us stronger in life.

Be Kind

Kindness can change the world. For real.

You have the power to impact your life...your workplace...and the world! That's not even an exaggeration.

In this context, being kind to your colleagues can 100%[4] deepen any connections you will make and connections you already have in place in the workplace. Why does that matter, though?

Your reputation. Being kind can be construed as being weak. *Well, it just isn't.* It takes so much more strength (especially during times of adversity) to be kind than to be a j*rk. It is very challenging to remain cordial and professional when someone is yelling at you or blaming you...but it is worth it. Also, avoid gossip at all costs as it can destroy your reputation the moment you utter it. It is never worth it to participate in that type of conversation. So, stay strong. Be kind, even when it is hard. Take the high road. There isn't much traffic there.

Your career. Those incredible connections you've made might eventually be your boss, or the CEO of another company looking to hire someone like you or someone that you will eventually supervise. Wouldn't it be great to have a positive connection with those people in case or when those situations come up in the future?

Your workplace. You can be the conductor of the

---

[4] Okay, maybe its 97% chance it will deepen your connections....regardless, we both know it certainly can't hurt to be kind at work, right?

kindness train. Your simple act of kindness – not what you say to someone, but how you say it – sets the kindness train into motion. You can be the positive change in your company's culture. Kindness breeds loyalty. Company cultures are no different...so let's train employees on kindness/integrity and make employees accountable for kindness as part of their annual performance reviews. It will make the company culture better and then employees will want to stay – which helps retain better employees and save the company money on their bottom line. That's right, kindness might even make your company some money – or least save it some money! Let's get that kindness train on the tracks!

Your values. Deep down we all know that we should be kind. Kindergartners learn this every single day at school – and somehow, we lose those principles as we grow older. Let's go back to what we learned as young kids. Just be kind. It's the right thing to do.

Yep, yep, kindness is awesome. And that sounds great in theory, but how? I'm so busy, I don't even have time to floss. Or make my lunch. Or dust my ceiling fans.[5] How can I make time to be kind to someone else? Here's how:

Open the door for someone.
Tell someone thank you for *just* doing their job.
Park between the lines.[6]
Offer a genuine compliment.
Hold the elevator door open as someone rushes to it.
Smile.
Encourage someone.
Share the best local restaurants with a new employee.

---
[5] Do people actually do that?

[6] Seriously. Can we all just park between the lines in the parking lot?

BRING IN DONUTS

Ask someone how they are doing.

After treating the other person with kindness, they will probably be pleasantly surprised by the act, and then will be *way* more likely to be kind to the next person who they interact with at work (or home). See the kindness train chugging along now?

Be kind. Work hard. Have fun.

Real Life Example

Here is a fun example of how I have connected with a colleague in the workplace.

Whipped Cream as a Coffee Lid.

The Background: If you couldn't already tell, I *love* sweets. Which is why you won't be surprised that this example involves a sweet treat. Obviously, I try to sneak something sweet into everything I eat and drink. Both at home and at work, I use an aerosol can of whipped cream to completely cover my cup of coffee. At first thought, it seems that the coffee is simply a vessel for whipped cream - and yes, that is correct. It is also a perfect lid for my coffee cup as I walk down the hall to my desk. Seriously! If you walk before it melts, it will prevent the coffee from sloshing outside of the cup. Mind...blown! Try it at home!

The Connection: As you can imagine, it is quite hilarious to watch a grown woman attempt to be a barista at the office kitchen. I'm always fumbling around with creamer, stevia packets and the coffee pot. After one of my colleagues watched me blunder around with my coffee a few times with an amused and bewildered face, I laughed out loud and told them why I was covering my coffee with a frothy layer of whipped cream. It was a two-minute conversation between people who worked in two entirely different departments. That conversation led to other casual conversations over the months and years. Fast forward a couple of years, and we ended up working together on a couple of projects. And voilà - we already had a connection so we didn't have to awkwardly get to know each other, which made it easier to move right into effectively communicating and collaborating together.

BRING IN DONUTS

Good stuff, my friends. Good stuff.

——

After reading this first section, it probably seemed like a lot of common sense. *And it is!!* Which is why it should be the easiest and yet one of the most important principles of any career strategy.

Connect with others.

Connect with them in an effective, easy, fun and productive way.

It will make you stand out – for all of the good reasons. It will make communicating and collaborating with you easier than with most other people in the workplace because you already have the connection down pat.

Whipped cream is the best coffee lid.

Communicate

How to communicate in a clear, concise and actionable way. Every single day.

We've connected. We established a relationship with one of our colleagues. That's fun.

Now it's time to master communication in the workplace. Let's go.

Communication is defined as: *the imparting or exchanging of information or news.*[7]

Every single day in the workplace we are *exchanging information* with colleagues. We are communicating all day long. If we can't properly communicate, we can't properly do our jobs. Thus, communication skills can make or break a career.

Additionally, the rationale behind each communication is crucial. Always know the reason why the communication is taking place. Before you initiate any communication, ask yourself, "What am I trying to accomplish?" Even chitchat should have a purpose, even if it's just to build camaraderie.

Give your audience the information they need, in the order they need it, in words designed to be clear and concise.

---

[7] By Merriam-Webster Dictionary.

Remember that every communication reflects upon your career. Emails/phone calls/meetings/voicemails – they all matter. They all add up to the sum of your career.

Every communication adds up to the sum of your career.

Be Honest

The foundation of every relationship[8] is trust.

In order to truly communicate with someone, you must be honest.

In order to truly succeed in your career, you must be honest.

Be honest with the other person.

Be honest with yourself.

Be Honest with Others. Workplace communication thrives on the concept of truth. The workplace is where we collect the insights of all of the employees in order to be productive and profitable as an organization. Answer difficult questions with the truth, even if it challenges the status quo.

It may not seem like a big deal in small doses, but lies can tear down an entire organization.

Let's refrain from telling someone what *we think* they want to hear. They need to hear the truth. Not an exaggeration of a harmless story or an exaggeration of data, but the actual truth. If you need to soften the message, then feel free to use a qualifier, such as;

- "It seems that..."
- "To me,..."
- "In my experience,..."; or

---

[8] All of those connections you made from the last section are now officially relationships - even if just casual ones around the donut box.

- "Based on what I've seen/experienced,..."

If you aren't telling the truth to others, then ask yourself some these (tough) questions[9] to get to the bottom of it:

- What are you hiding?
- What are you afraid of?
- Are you trying to impress them?
- Are you trying to fit in?
- Are you feeling vulnerable?
- How can you value something or be valued when it is based on a lie?

That being said, being honest doesn't give you a green light to speak in an unfiltered, rude or gossipy. If speaking the truth makes the hair on your neck stand straight up or gives you the hives, double check your intention - is that in the right place? Are you trying to embarrass someone or simply make yourself look good in spite of someone else? *Be truthful and tactful.*

Be Honest with Yourself. Can you really do what is being asked of you? Can you really meet the deadline that was given to you – or the deadline you self-imposed? If not, then speak up, my friend!!

Be Honest on Your Resume/LinkedIn Profile. Just make sure these statements are truthful. Lies on these

---

[9] In all seriousness, I can't even pretend to have all of the answers to these tough questions. However, it's a good exercise to consider the root cause of why it's hard to tell the truth in certain circumstances.

items can have dire circumstances, such as not being able to do a job that you said you have done in the past or not passing a background check!!!

Sleep Better. Let's be honest[10], you can sleep WAY better if you have lived your day – and your life – in an honest way.

If that wasn't enough to remind us to tell the truth, let's end with the definition and origin of honest:

- Honest is defined as: *free from fraud or deception*[11]

- Origin and etymology of honest[12]: Middle English, from Anglo-French, from Latin *honestus* honorable, from *honos*, honor.

Let's simplify it even more:

Fraud or Deception ≠ Honor

Honesty is the best foundation to every successful career.

---

[10] Pun intended there.

[11] By Merriam-Webster Dictionary.

[12] By Merriam-Webster Dictionary.

Be Respectful

What does being respectful look like?

Respectfulness is when you believe that the other person is worthy of your time and insights.

Respectfulness is when you admire the qualities and capabilities of the other person.

Many of the things we have already covered in this book constitute being respectful, such as being kind, being honest and actively listening. But let's delve deeper into this notion of respect and how it can help you communicate. Respecting others, in every way, will lead to more effective communications while building stronger relationships, gaining more trust and understanding your colleague's needs. Respect is the cornerstone of an open line of communication.

Be respectful of etiquette. Please. Thank You. Proper spelling. Using manners in this fast-paced world will truly set you apart from others in the workplace. People will remember the pleasant, albeit perhaps old fashioned in some people's minds, way of communicating that you regularly bring to the workplace.

Be respectful of time. Be on time. Whether it is for a meeting or for a project deadline, be on time. Other people have just as busy lives, yet somehow, they make it on time. Completing tasks on time showcases that you are an employee who can be trusted and held accountable. Therefore, please, manage your time accordingly. If you can't make a deadline or an obligation, then let someone know well before it is due, so that some of the obligations can be properly delegated.

Be respectful of space. Close-talker, this one is for you. Please know that everyone has a different sized personal bubble. Mine, for instance, is quite large. Others are nearly invisible. If you see someone slowly moving backwards while you talk with them in person...then please step it back a notch. This doesn't necessarily mean they don't like you[13], it means their personal bubble has been punctured and needs to filled back up again. Additionally, please refrain from stretching your arm across someone's face to point at the monitor. This is uncomfortable for some people – okay, it's me again. Finally, please don't walk behind someone's desk to point at a screen, grab a pencil, look at a picture, etc. – again, this one is me.[14] When a personal-space-invader is headed into the bubble, communication ceases to exist – again, maybe this is just me.

Be respectful of pronouns.[15] *Pronouns can be the scariest words in the workplace.* Refrain from using pronouns while communicating. Pronouns tend to make the communication into a blame game. "You said..." or "I told you to..." or "Remember when you did..." "Why didn't you...?" Those pronouns literally make the hairs stand up on my neck. Here some ways to avoid them:

- Hairs Stand Up on Neck: *You told me* _____ .

---

[13] Although, it could, but let's look at the glass half-full here.

[14] If I'm alone in the concern of personal space invaders, I apologize for taking your time on that one. Just needed to get that one off of my chest.

[15] One of my favorite pieces of advice. If you use a highlighter when reading books, then you might want to highlight this section.

- Neck Hairs Stay Where They Need To Be: *As discussed, _____.*

- Hairs Stand Up on Neck: *I asked you to _____.*
- Neck Hairs Stay Where They Need To Be: *Per our chat, _____.*

- Hairs Stand Up on Neck: *Why did you do that?*
- Neck Hairs Stay Where They Need To Be: *Seeking some clarity on how things were handled.*

Be respectful of absolutes. "Never say never." "Always is a long time." These were some my Dad's favorite things to tell us when we were kids. He was correct in steering me from using absolutes in my communications with others. Using absolutes can make you look unrefined and impractical while also shutting down the communication lines because you have made no room for another consideration. The only absolute that is acceptable is to say that we should never use absolutes.

Be respectful of ideas. Whether it is due to arrogance or insecurity – which can be the same thing – don't let your own ideas get in the way of the ideas of others. Be open to other ideas, concepts and procedures. Your openness will breed more open communication because you have set the stage for bringing more than one idea to the table.

Let's respect each other, so that our communication can thrive!

In order to get respect, you must earn respect.

Ask the Right Questions

We all know that there aren't any dumb questions. Or so our parents and teachers tell us...yet, I think the jury is still out on this adage.

But do you know that in the workplace there are questions – and then there are the right questions?

Regular questions are great, especially when we are trying to connect with someone. They show curiosity and embrace the idea of seeking to understand.

The right questions, though. That is where your career will soar, your communication style will flourish and your reputation will launch in new ways. The right questions lead discussions to areas far beyond the current thinking and give people permission to think outside of the box.

While preparing for your next meeting or conversation, bring some thoughtful questions that will generate productive and innovative communication.

One more quick thing: Before you start generating a list of the right questions, check your motive for asking them: Are you just trying to snag some attention and seem intelligent? Or do you genuinely have a question that will move the conversation forward? Only you will know the answer to that.

Here are some examples of some regular questions[16] vs. the right questions when communicating in the workplace:

---

[16] Questions are great. Even if they may not seem like the right questions. It still turns conversations on their side, which is a good thing!

Question: Why are we doing this?

Right question: Would you please provide some background information, so we can put this into context?

Boom. You are basically asking for them to give you the entire back story, so that you can put the pieces together of this puzzle. Brilliant.

Question: Can you get this done?

Right question: What is the goal of this project?

Define the end goal in order to be able to work effectively towards that well-defined end goal. Seeking clarity is key to any communication, so this question gets to the heart of the intention of the project.

Question: Why are we doing this?

Right question: How does this support our goal?

Once you have defined a goal, you can double check every step along the way to make sure it is aligned with the end goal. It's a form of checks and balances that every organization needs to maintain effectiveness and efficiency.

Question: What if we fail?

Right question: What are the consequences of doing this? Are there consequences beyond the short and mid-term?

Let's think about the consequences beyond just the short term – and really brainstorm what would happen if we go through with this project. This is a hard question to answer, but that is why the question needs to be asked...and you will look amazing by being the one to ask the tough question.

Question: How much money will we make?

Right question: What will success look like for this project? Is it something other than just financial success?

Sometimes, money is the driving force behind decisions. Sometimes, money is not the right reason to complete a project. There might be ethical reasons to do something differently. There might be intangible values that haven't been considered yet. Be the one to bring those to the conversation.

Question: Can your department own this?

Right question: Who else should be involved in this decision/project?

Selectively bringing in other departments or people into the conversation can lead to impactful insights and drive a project to completion without missing important steps. That being said, make sure there are not too many cooks in the kitchen...but make sure there are a few sous chefs to take it from a fast food meal to a five-star meal.

Question: Any questions?

Right question: Are we asking the right questions?

When you are asked if there are any questions, typically it will be met with an uncomfortable silence, or, equally uncomfortable, the same person asking more questions to just hear themselves talk. However, if you are asked this question, it might stop you in your tracks, and force you to really wonder if the right questions are being asked. Mind. Blown.

Question: What do you think?

Right question: May we have your opinion or insights on this?

People want to be recognized and seen. Even if they are quiet during a meeting or discussion. The way this is phrased, it gives them the option not to answer at this current moment – this gives them an out, in case they need a few moments/days to properly craft their response. For our amazing introverts, it might provide them with more confidence to give their opinion. Yes!

Bonus right question: Is there anything else I can help you with?

YES!! You have just solidified your connection, opened the lines of communication AND became more accountable with one simple question. Nice work, my friend. One, it shows that you think like a team member. Two, it shows that you are open to working on what's best for the organization, even if it is beyond your stated job duties.

Use these types of questions to help your organization improve their productivity, to facilitate better conversations and to make your reputation stand out as an innovative employee. How does that sound?[17]

Asking the right questions forces people to think outside the box. Outside the box is where brilliance exists.

---

[17] Did you see what I did there? Asked a question at the end of a section on questions. ☺

Be Clear and Concise

Despite our best efforts, none of us are mind-readers. Others don't know what we need from them, unless we tell them – and tell them in a *clear and concise way*.

Clear. Crystal clear. What is the reason you are communicating with the other person? If you aren't clear on the rationale, then the other person won't be either.

Statements and requests that are ambiguous, vague, convoluted or complex will instantly put a block in the lines of communication. It forces people to read between the lines or connect the dots in order to comprehend what you are trying to communicate. It will add extra steps in order to clear up the confusion. Those extra steps can add minutes, hours, days or weeks to remove the confusion and get back on track.

Concise. Less is more. Get right to the point. Remove unnecessary adjectives. Summarizing is a great thing to do at the end of the communication, but try to avoid repeating yourself several times throughout the conversation/communication. Repeating yourself more than once becomes redundant and makes you seem less articulate.

Let's remember that every single person has many things going on in their jobs at one time. While you may have a specific question or request in mind for a few minutes, hours or days – the other person may not have the same context or background when you send them information or a request. So, please be crystal clear and concise as to <u>what you need and why</u> you are reaching out to them – during every single interaction. Make it easy for them to help you.

What exactly do you need from the other person?

Do you need:

- To share information
  - This would be an FYI (For Your Information).
  - <u>The FYI acronym is often improperly used in workplace communication.</u> Often someone will say FYI, but they really want the other person to take some action. However, if it says, FYI – then that's what it should mean – that it is simply information for the other person. If you want the other person to do actually something with the information, then ask them!
- To receive information
  - This would be a *specific* request.
  - This could take the form of a:
    - Question
      - Could you please[18] provide a status of the _____ project[19]?
      - Who should take the lead on this project?
    - Request to take action
      - Can you please send me this month's report?

---

[18] Notice the manners – even when asking for something from a colleague. Manners go a long way, my friends!

[19] Use descriptive words to define what project you are talking about - most people have more than one project going on at one time.

- Can you please complete the attached survey?
    - Request to stop doing something
        - Would you please hold off on paying that supplier until you hear otherwise?
        - Please stop working on this project until you hear otherwise.

In order to avoid any confusion, let's be clear and concise - every single time we communicate. Doing this will benefit your colleagues, will provide productivity to your organization and will make you look awesome!! Wouldn't it be great if whenever someone receives a communication from you – they don't dread it – because they know you will not waste anyone's time? Bravo, my friend!

Let them know what you need - it will benefit everyone involved!

Provide The Right Amount of Information.

At this point in your communication, you've been honest, respectful and asked the right questions while being clear and concise. What now? Now it is more of an art than a science. Give your colleagues the right amount of information. Not too much and not too little. Enough for them to proceed with the project, but not too much to bore them and not too little that they need to continue to seek more information.

Look to the other person for guidance on how much information to provide:

- Did they ask you a yes/no question? If at all possible, answer it with a yes or no answer. If there needs to be additional clarification, then keep it limited to what is needed for the specific question asked of you; OR

- Did they ask you an open-ended question? The amount of information provided on this answer will depend on the audience. If the other person has lots of background information on the particular question, then less is more. If the other person doesn't have a lot of background information on the particular question, then provide enough context to give them the answer but don't overwhelm them with unnecessary details.

It is important to focus on the most relevant background information and details. More than that, and it is simply an ineffective way to communicate.

And just like that, we don't need to give any more information on this topic.

The gift of less words.

Giving the right amount of information can shave hours off of each project.

Know Your Audience

Oh, my friends. This tip is a little-known secret in the workplace.

This is probably one of my favorite tips of all time. This particular skill took me several years to master and I learned it the hard way. Hopefully this simple and effective communicate skill will skyrocket your career!!

What does it mean to know your audience? It means to cater your communication to the other person's preferences. Let's consider these types of factors:

Department/Role. What department do they work in?

- If they are a finance person, speak to them in numbers – quantify things for them.
- If they are an HR person, use stories.
- If they are a legal person, provide substantiation to back up all statements.
- If they are an operations person, reference what part of the process/procedure is impacted.

Timing. When is the best time to approach them?

- Are they morning people or evening people?
- If they are morning people, then schedule meetings with them first thing in the morning – and avoid asking them to make tough decisions later in the day.
- If they are evening people, don't schedule an 8am meeting and expect a good result.

- Do they eat lunch in the office or out of the office? If they eat out of the office most days, then don't schedule a 12:30pm meeting.

Communication Style. How do they prefer to communicate?

- Do they prefer emailing about everything? Or do they prefer talking in person? Some people are visual people and some people are auditory people.
- Do they prefer to have a meeting for every topic? If so, schedule fifteen minute meetings, so as to save everyone else's schedule.
- Do they like people to pop in with questions? If so, then take advantage of it. If not, then send an email or call them to set them up for the question/request, so they can be properly prepared to talk about it.

How do you find out about these preferences/styles?

- Ask them. This is my favorite way to discover my audience's preferences/styles. Just ask them. Let them know that you want to make it easier on them, so you are wondering what the best way is to communicate with them. Often, they have never been asked that question – and it will make them feel remarkable that you care about them and it will make you look tremendous because you actually do care about them.

Let me assure you that understanding your audience will put you light years ahead in your career. It will lend itself to getting better responses in a more efficient way and it

BRING IN DONUTS

will ensure that your communication lines aren't clogged with frustrated people who wish they were better understood.

Know your audience. For example, if you are talking to finance, talk to them using numbers.

Follow-up/Finish

Like every good story, communications need a beginning, a middle and an ending. You've started a communication, you've asked for what you needed, you've been asked for what others needed – now what? Now, we close the loop. We summarize and finish up the project/matter.

Doesn't that just happen organically? Maybe, maybe not. If a communication is over, doesn't it just end? Sometimes there are leaders who drive projects and communications in a way that is crystal clear that everyone's roles/inputs are completed. Far more often, it is unclear if everything is wrapped up...and it can come back to haunt people in a few days, weeks, months or years!

Here's how to avoid that situation:

If you are the initiator of the communication/request/project. Once the communication and/or project is completed, tell everyone involved two things:

1. *Thank you for your insights/thoughts/ideas/contributions/etc.*[20] This acknowledges that you appreciate any time and effort they have given to this project.

2. *If we need anything else, we will be in touch.* This allows the other person to put this matter in their archives, unless they hear back from you. It is clear that the ball is in your court, not theirs. They can let out a small sigh of relief. They are released.

---

[20] And really mean it...look to the section on gratitude for more on this topic.

If you are the recipient of the communication/request/project. Once you have completely responded to the initiator, tell them two things:

1. *Hope this is what you needed.* This allows the other person to know that there is always room for improvement and that you are open to additional requests/comments.

2. *Please let me know if you need anything else.* This allows you to put this matter in your archives, unless you hear back from them. It is clear that the ball is in their court, not yours. You can let out a small sigh of relief. You are released.

Following up and finalizing the communication is like putting a big red bow on it. It signals completion and allows everyone to be fully informed of the final status. It is a true and rare gift in the workplace. Give the gift of completion. It never expires.

Proactively communicating that a project is completed is like putting a big red bow on it.

Practical Tips

We've covered a lot in this section. What does effective communication look like from a practical perspective? I'm so glad you asked...here are a few ways to apply these communication tips:

In Person

Communicating in person has so many benefits:

Body language. You can observe the way the person is physically responding to the conversation. Are they happy, sad, frustrated, indifferent or something else? With that crucial insight, you can tailor the rest of the conversation with them.

Quick. If you have the right amount of time to talk with someone in person, you can eliminate an unnecessary email or meeting. Bonus!

Emotional. Communicating in person is the best avenue for any news that would be construed as slightly emotional. Do you have great news to share about the profits of the company? Tell them in person – then you can savor the positive enthusiasm with them at the same time. Do you have constructive news to give about their performance? Tell them in person – then you can answer their immediate questions in real time and it doesn't make you look indifferent or like someone hiding behind a screen.

Communicating in person also has some cautionary tales:

- **The ol' drop ins.** Despite many people's proud announcement that they have an "Open Door Policy" - this may not always be true. In theory,

BRING IN DONUTS

they truly, *truly* mean it. In practicality, it's a really hard policy to uphold. Be careful when you just drop in on someone during the workday – in fact, check their calendar to see if they are busy. If their calendar is booked, then there is probably a good reason – and even more of a reason for you not to just bop in. More often than not, they will be in the middle of a thought, a project, a conference call, an email or one of a million other things. Even if there isn't someone else at their desk, you might still be interrupting them. While you may have been thinking about this topic for moments, minutes, hours or days – when you pop in on someone, they won't have that same thought process and will need to be caught up to where you are in your mind. Please just remember that. Here's how to avoid those awkward situations:

- "Hi Jimmy![21] Do you have a moment?" This is perfect.
  - If they say yes, then use all of the tools we have discussed in this section on communication. Give them any corresponding background information, the current information they need, in the order they need it – and in a clear and concise way, along with what you need from them.
  - If they say no, then say, "Okay, thanks. I'll be in touch." *And don't take offense,*

---

[21] This is CRUCIAL. Use a salutation and their name. It makes it personal. It doesn't just bombard them with the content you want to share with them. It eases them into a conversation. Don't forget the salutation and their name!

because you have been kind, polite and professional. Then email them – or set up a meeting while considering their communication preferences/styles you've ascertained (see page 51[22]).

- **Close-talker.** Please see page 39.

Meetings

When held effectively, meetings can be incredible uses of people's time. Sadly, often they can be a waste of everyone's time. Here's a list of what to do when you are about to schedule a meeting:

1. **Intent.** Why do you need this meeting? Can it be handled via email or a quick phone call instead?
2. **People.** Who *truly* needs to be part of this meeting? Is it the seventeen people you have in mind – or maybe just a solid four people? Does it need to be with the leaders who can cascade it to their teams? Or is it with the people doing the day-to-day operations and they can FYI their supervisors after the meeting?
3. **Length.** Does this meeting need to be one hour or a mere fifteen minutes? If held efficiently and effectively, most meetings can be done in less than thirty minutes.
4. **Agenda/Invitation.** On the calendar invite, give everyone the appropriate background information, including *exactly why* this meeting is being held. Provide an agenda in the meeting notice of who will

---

[22] Isn't this getting exciting?! Using these skills have practical applications that you can use today!!!

be there, the project name and the goals of the meeting.

5. **Meeting Notes.** Whoever called the meeting should take meticulous notes. If they aren't able to take notes, then they should delegate it to someone else. Here are some examples of great meeting notes:

- What – Topic of the Meeting
- Why – Why Was the Meeting Called
- Who – Who Was in the Meeting
- Action Items with Due Dates – Detailed Action Items Assigned to Individuals – and *when* they are due
- Next Steps – What are the Next Steps to Accomplish the Goal(s)
- Owner – Who Will Follow-Up on the Action Items and Next Steps

6. **Donuts.** Are donuts needed at the meeting? A crucial step to consider in all meetings.

7. **Follow-up.** The scribe of the meeting should send out the meeting notes that highlight the action items and next steps. The owner of the meeting is responsible for continuing to drive this project/goal until completion. Once the project/goal is completed or over, then the owner must communicate that to the others.

Bam. You've just held a productive and effective meeting. Nice job.

Emails

These days, emails are often the preferred form of communication in the workplace. Emails allow you to be articulate, clear and concise. Emails are also a great way to document the current status of a project.

To be honest, emails are one of my favorite ways to communicate in the workplace. I use emails as a to-do list.[23] In fact, if someone tells me in person that they need something (and I don't have a notebook in hand[24]), I ask them to send me a quick email, so that I better keep track of what is being requested of me.

Here are some easy and actionable tips to make your emails exceptional:

Wait. If you are sending an email and you are mad/frustrated/annoyed/feeling sassy, *please* wait to send it. Wait until you are no longer emotional. If you can't get over your frustration, then email isn't the right avenue to communicate. Pick up the phone, or even better, talk to them in person. Remember, whatever you put in an email can virtually last forever, long after you've gotten over whatever temporary bad feeling you had when you sent it.

Intent. Why do you need to send this email? What is the goal of this email? Is it information or a request for something?

People. Who *truly* needs to be on this email? Is it the forty-three people you have in mind – or maybe just three people? Are the other forty people needed on the cc line –

---

[23] This is a definite personal preference. Some people frown upon this way of using emails. I smile upon this way of using emails. Regardless, do what is best for you!

[24] Which is frankly, quite rare. Tip: Always have a notebook and pen for these exact situations. It will allow you to keep track of what was discussed.

or can you trust that the three people will cascade the information/request accordingly?

Forwarding emails. While there is information below, restate a summary for the recipients rather than just making them decipher it. Save them time and make yourself look astounding. Please don't just forward an email without any commentary above the forwarded email. *Please.*

Structure. Use a structured template for sending emails.

- **If you are the initiator of the communication/request/project:**
    - Subject lines are your friends.
    - Salutation + Greeting
        - Say hello! And use their name(s)!
        - Use some type of relevant greeting: Hope all is well! or Happy Monday[25]!
    - Content
        - Confidential and Proprietary. Make sure that what you send via email isn't confidential or proprietary – and can be shared with the recipients.
        - Use bullet points or short sentences. This makes it way easier to read. When you see eleven lines of text with no break, do you want to delve into that text? Probably not.
        - PRONOUNS! Please refrain from using them, if at all possible.

---

[25] Is this a thing? I really want it to be a thing, but I'm not sure Mondays are always super happy.

- Start with a quick summary of the information or request, <u>along with a due date</u>. When there is a due date, use one of the fancy font types to help emphasize the date - **bold can feel like yelling**, *italics can feel like formal emphasis* and <u>underlines feel ro-bo-tic</u>. Or maybe that's just how I feel...
- Provide concise and appropriate background information, depending on recipient list.
- Repeat the information or request.
- Gratitude + Closing
    - Say thank you!
- Attachments. Save the files with a name that is easy to understand. Example: CompanyA_CompanyB Agreement (fully signed) 060118.pdf[26]

- **If you are the recipient of the communication/request/project:**
    - <u>Reply all – cautionary tale</u>
        - We all know someone (or maybe ourselves) who has a reply all story. They are horrific stories. Stuff of legends.

---

[26] This is a tip you can implement today and it will save the recipient SO much frustration. They can instantly know what is in the file, rather than guess what "x90073cw357b.doc" means.

- Salutation + Greeting
    - Say hello! And use their name(s)!
    - Use some type of relevant greeting - it doesn't have to be a question: Hope your Tuesday is going well! Hope you are staying warm in this weather!
- Don't make it seem like they are inconveniencing you: "Happy to help...."
- Answer the question. Or seek clarity, if it isn't clear (or they haven't read page 46).
    - Confidential and Proprietary. Make sure that what you send via email isn't confidential or proprietary - and can be shared with the recipients.
    - PRONOUNS! Please refrain from using them, if at all possible.
    - Use bullet points or short sentences. This makes it way easier to read. When you see eleven lines of text with no break, do you want to delve into that text? Probably not.
    - If you can't answer the question or provide the documentation they need - <u>give them a *realistic* timeline and then abide by that timeline.</u>
- Gratitude + Closing
    - Say thank you!
- Attachments. Save the files with a name that is easy to understand. Example: CompanyA_CompanyB Agreement (fully

Phone calls

Sometimes phone calls are a great way to communicate. They can shave off days of responding to emails, if used properly. Here are some ways to properly communicate via phone calls:

- Salutation - Say hello and *use their name.*
  - "Hi Jimmy."
- Ask if they have a moment to chat. Be courteous. The person you've called may be in the middle of a huge project and a complicated story/question may not be good timing.
  - "Do you have a moment to chat?"
    - If the answer is no, then ask: "When is a good time to chat?"
- Tell them if you are asking them a question or giving them information. This will properly frame the phone call.
- Give them a bit a background information in order to give them context.
  - DO NOT start mid-sentence with a story that you assume they know already.
- Ask the question/share the information.
- Send a follow-up email if there is an action item for either of you.

It probably sounds more complicated than it is in practice, but these tips will help you to avoid ann*ying a colleague with a frustrating phone call.

Voicemail - *Can we please limit these to less than 30 seconds. Please?*

Voicemails are no different than any other communication. Just a super shortened version of them.

Be clear and concise. Please. This is a personal request as well. When I see the red dot on the desk phone, my heart skips a beat. Mostly because it requires me to have a notepad to keep detailed notes from a person speaking so quickly that I can barely keep up with their voicemail. Just be clear and concise. That's all.

Here's an example:

"Hi Jimmy. This is Jamie. I have a quick question for you about _____ (concise summary). Please give me a call at xxx-xxx-xxxx. Again, this is Jamie at xxx-xxx-xxxx. Thanks and have a great day."

Ta-da!!

Real life Examples

Legal Department Reputation.

Once upon a time, there was a legal department that may or may not have had a bad reputation. Wait a minute...that could be nearly every legal department in nearly every organization – despite how great the attorneys are within the legal department! Let's try this one again.

Once upon a time, there was a legal department that was poorly perceived by other departments in the organization. The legal department was sad about their reputation and wanted to improve their reputation, while helping the other departments in a more effective way. It was clear that the lines of communication were part of what was causing the bad reputation.

Since the workload wasn't going to improve and the number of lawyers wasn't going to increase, one of the legal eagles had an idea! Let's improve our communication! But how? Simple!

The legal eagle made one *small, easy* tweak to her daily communications. It was quick and free to make the change. In response to every email request that would take more than a few hours to review, here is what the legal eagle emailed:

"Hi Jamie,

Thanks for your email. *I'll review and be in touch*.

Have a great day~

Legal Eagle"

That super simple daily email did it! It changed the perception of the legal department. But why? Because it is:

- **Honest.** It lets them know you will be in touch. It doesn't give a timeframe, but it is honest in that you will be in touch.
- **Respectful.** It responds to their email in a timely way. You have been respectful of their timeframe.
- **Clear and Concise.** It is crystal-clear that you received the email and will be in touch. It doesn't give weird excuses or explanations as to why you can't review it right now. It's concise.

Isn't it great when tips can be applied in real life?! Yay!!

Honestly, respect and clarity will enhance any communication.

Collaborate

How to play well with your colleagues - and still get the job done.

We have connected and effectively communicated. And that's terrific. Isn't that all there is to succeeding at the workplace? Not even close, my friends.

This is where the magic begins - where the collision of established connections and effective communications becomes a burst of brilliant collaboration.

Let's collaborate in a way that helps improve the bottom line, increase productivity and advances your reputation.

In six-year-old terms, let's play nicely together.

Collaboration doesn't always have a start and an end. Sometimes it is just the daily acts of working together as a team, department and organization.

Collaboration is the magic of every successful career.

Be Prepared

Preparation is a lot like discipline. It isn't very exciting, but when applied to your daily workplace tasks, those seeds of preparation will blossom into a sensational career. One day at a time. One interaction at a time. One collaboration at a time.

Being prepared as an individual is great.

But being prepared when working with others is incredible. It benefits the individuals, the group and the organization.

Collaboration thrives when the individuals and the group are prepared. Consider all of the successful sports teams out there. They didn't just get to become champions out of sheer luck or barely training. They prepared individually by taking care of themselves. They prepared as a group by working together, despite the different styles of the individuals. Without preparation, they would look like a bunch of six-year-olds running around a soccer field[27].

Being prepared can take on two different approaches:

Physical preparation.

- Write a daily checklist – *the night before*. That way you won't forget about any important tasks that might be overlooked after a relaxing evening and a restful slumber.[28]

---

[27] Imagine eight kids swarming after the ball, but no one knowing what to do with the ball once they get to it. The other two kids are twirling or picking flowers. That's what your workplace will look like if people aren't prepared before they collaborate on a project. Do we really want people twirling around in the hallways? Maybe, but probably not.

[28] Here's hoping you get relaxing evenings and restful slumbers. That

- Gather documents/materials the day before the meeting/event. That way you can see if you are missing something with plenty of time to find it or create it.

- Read the materials/emails *before* the next meeting. Take notes while you read the materials. Propose questions/ideas while you are reading the materials. That way you won't have to play catch up, while wasting everyone else's valuable time (who *did* read the materials before the meeting). Also, it makes you look remarkable if you can already be up to speed before the meeting starts because then you can ask the *right* questions - see how this is all coming together - it is very exciting stuff! It can help your colleagues by being able to answer their questions.

Mental preparation. This one is WAY harder.

- Are you ready and willing to work with your colleagues?

- Are you able to check your personal stuff at the door before you embark on this project?

- Are you able to get past the quirks of your colleagues to be able to see the value that they bring to every situation?

- After you answer yes to these, then mentally organize your thoughts, so they are aligned with the goal of the collaboration.

Being prepared isn't easy, it isn't thrilling and it may not always get noticed. But being unprepared will make you

---

sounds amazing and something to strive for in the years ahead (coming from a mom with three young kids).

stand out in all the wrong ways – every, single time.

Be the most prepared. It will always be a terrific use of your time.

Anticipate Questions/Bring Solutions

This tip is like a little magic trick that you can put to use today – and every day. And then watch the magic happen...

Before we get to this little magic trick, let's remember that collaborating with others requires us to think about the other person. People want to be understood and heard.

When you work with someone over a period of time, pay attention to make sure you hear them. You can do this by noticing the following: *What types of questions do they ask?* It's that simple. *What types of questions do they ask?*

Let's go a step further with this idea of helping the other person – I promise we will get to the magic – what are the workplace problems that are keeping them up at night? You can do this by noticing the following during your interactions: *What is their perpetual concern in situations?* That perspective will showcase what concerns they have on an ongoing basis or on a particular project.

...the magic is coming...

Now what?! Okay, here goes nothing:

Anticipate Their Questions.

- You've been taking notes. You've been listening. You've noticed their style of communication.
- Jimmy always asks how much this will cost. *SO BE READY FOR THAT QUESTION.* Before he even asks the question, mention that it will cost $_____.

- Jamie always asks what we've done in the past in these types of situations. *SO BE READY FOR THAT QUESTION.* Before she even asks the question, mention that in the past we have done _____.

- Jimmy Jr. always asks why would we want to do this thing. *SO BE READY FOR THAT QUESTION.* Before he even asks the question, mention that the rationale for this is _____.

- <u>IT'S MAGIC!</u> You've successfully anticipated their questions. They will be insanely impressed. And you will look phenomenal because you have helped them, your organization and yourself.

Bring Solutions.

- Same story as anticipating questions: You've been taking notes. You've been listening. You've noticed their style of communication.

- Example: There is always a problem of getting the projects done quickly. Before you meet, create an aggressive timeline that all participants can sign off on and will be accountable to during the project.

- Example: There is always a problem of an unclear process. Before you meet, draft a simple process that all participants can sign off on and will be accountable to during the project.

- <u>IT'S MAGIC!</u> You've successfully brought solutions to the problems that will inevitably be discussed. Even if the team doesn't agree with your proposed solution, at least you will be respected for trying to bring solutions to the table – and not just problems. Once again, you have helped them, your organization and yourself.

Be proud of yourself. You've just jumped a few rungs up on the corporate ladder by implementing these tips. And you learned a new magic trick that didn't require you to borrow a white rabbit.

Anticipate questions. Bring solutions. And watch your career soar!

Be Resourceful

When working with others, please don't work with blinders on. Help your colleagues find answers or help them find the right person with the answers. It doesn't take much time and that colleague may be willing to help you someday in unexpected ways.

Throughout your career, there will be many times when people ask you for something (as part of collaborating) and you simply don't have the answer. There are two options at that point: 1. Telling them no and going on your merry little way; OR 2. *Help them* find the answer or *help them* find the person with the answer. Which of those two options is the best for your colleague, the best for your organization and the best for your reputation/career?[29]

For simplicity's sake, let's assume that all of you picked option #2. Good choice! For those that picked option #2 with some hesitation, let's dive into this a bit deeper to see the value of it. Helping someone to find the answer or find the person with the answer will take very little of your time in the grand scheme of your career. Often it would be a matter of picking up the phone to see if someone else has the document, or looking in a file cabinet[30], or checking the server or sending a quick email to someone to ask for their assistance. Even if it takes you fifteen minutes of your day, this simple action will truly set you apart from other colleagues.

---

[29] Imagine a famous game show's final segment music playing while you genuinely consider these options.

[30] Are these still part of the workplace? Or are they considered vintage now?

Let's take a moment to see what a small world it is – and how helping a colleague can help our career.

Several years ago, I interviewed at a Fortune 500 company. It was a wonderful group of people whom I had the opportunity to interview with at the company. After careful consideration with my husband, I *respectfully* declined the offer. Fast forward a few years...the same woman who offered me a job at that Fortune 500 company was now interviewing to become my new boss at a different Fortune 500 company! She is awesome and eventually became my boss. The moral of the story is that if I had not *respectfully* declined that offer – and been a j*rk about it – then my career at the new company could have been compromised by my own doing. Instead, we were thrilled to work together and she has become my trusted mentor and dear friend.

No matter what industry you work in or what type of job you have, the world is much smaller than we all think. That person you were rude to in the office might eventually be your spouse's boss (work parties will become *awkward*). That neighbor who you cut off in the cul-de-sac might eventually be your customer or supplier (asking for favors from that person will definitely not happen). Let's look at the flip side of that coin, let's say you've been incredibly resourceful with one of your current colleagues, they appreciated it and yet didn't make a big deal about it. Fast forward a few years and now you are interviewing for a position and they have some leverage in that decision because they are now a leader in your company. Your resourcefulness will play a part in their decision whether to hire you for the role.

Being resourceful reaches its extreme value when people collaborate as a team, share their insights and use it for good.

Go above and beyond for your colleagues. It's helpful, courteous and makes a difference.

Work Hard

Blah, blah, work hard, blah, blah. Is that what it looked like when you read the title of this section? Please bear with me on this one.

Working hard as an individual is one thing. You should work hard – but only as hard as you want to succeed[31]. It's like your own report card. You are the one responsible for it, no one else.

Working hard as part of a group is a whole 'nother[32] ballgame. It's a requirement. Other people are counting on you to pull your weight. A team can't win the game if one of the players isn't working hard during the entire game. The same goes for working together in the workplace. Projects can't succeed if one of the colleagues isn't working hard during the entire process.

Here are some great ways to work harder for you and your team:

Focus on the end. Once you are done with all of the hard work, you will be done working so hard. Is that enough motivation? Sometimes seeing the light at the end of the tunnel is enough for me to work super hard to be done with it. We know that there will be more hard work after the light at the end of the tunnel, but who wants to focus on the negative? That's boring. And sad.

---

[31] This is not a PSA for not working hard as an individual. It is just a reminder that each of us has our own work ethic for our individual work, some may just be more aggressive than others.

[32] I just like the way " 'nother" sounds. It's not grammatically correct, but it is exactly how I would say it if we were talking in person.

Bite-sized pieces. Basically, donut holes. Eating an entire donut may seem like too many calories or too filling[33]. But popping down a few donut holes is way easier to digest – especially if you space it out throughout the day/week. So, let's view this workload as a giant bear claw donut that can't be done all at once. Let's break it up into 5 tiny, delicious and amazing glaze-covered donut holes. You can do the work one donut hole at a time. Easier to digest. Easy peasy, donut pleasey.

Easy, Easy, Hard. Do two easy tasks, then one hard task. That way you can knock a few things out and feel accomplished before you tackle a tougher task. Starting with a hard task can seem daunting, so get some momentum before you tackle it.

Closing time. When is the due date? Work backwards from the due date. If you think it will take 2 hours to get it done, then plan accordingly – and leave some time for the inevitable mistakes/problems that may rise while working on it.

In summary, blah, blah, blah, work hard, blah, blah, blah.

Work hard. Blah. Blah. While not too exciting, it actually works in transforming your career.

---

[33] I mean, that doesn't ever happen to me. But it's my understanding that it happens to most normal people who consume donuts.

Be Accountable/Expect Accountability

Being accountable means you have to get your stuff done and take responsibility for what you did get done.

Every single person in an organization, from the executives to the interns contribute to the success (and challenges) of the organization. Each individual needs to take responsibility for their actions - good and bad.

Accountability isn't about a blame game or finger-pointing if something goes wrong[34]. It is about being honest, true to your word and standing by your outputs.

What accountability looks like in the workplace:

- Performing the responsibilities of the employee's role
- Completing the assignments given to the employee within their own control
- Working with colleagues towards a collective goal for the organization

If those items aren't clear, then immediately seek clarity as to what your job function is and what assignments you need to complete and in what timeframe.

If those items aren't done properly and in a timely fashion, the employee can expect corresponding consequences which might be as extreme as being terminated.[35]

---

[34] At least it shouldn't be about a blame game. If it is at your organization, then present your concerns with the appropriate leaders to let them know what the perception is of accountability as an organization. If they aren't receptive, then find another leader who will listen...and keep asking until you find someone who will listen to your concerns.

Therefore, if you are having trouble understanding your responsibilities, completing your assignments or working with others - ask for help! Sooner rather than later. *Be accountable for yourself.* No one can read your mind to know if you are overwhelmed or drowning in fear/work. *Be accountable for your own actions* and get the assistance you need to get your job done. Even if it is an uncomfortable conversation to ask for help or express concern in your abilities, it will be *way* less uncomfortable than if you are having a conversation in the future with someone due to your lack of performance.

Let's remember something terrific: You already have built valuable connections and have learned how to communicate effectively with them. Therefore, you have tools to talk to someone about the items you are accountable for in the organization. This will help tremendously for any tough conversation.

What does accountability have to do with collaboration? Here's a quick analogy: Remember those group projects you had to do in elementary school. The ones where you were so pumped when Jimmy was in your group, because he did all the work every time – since he wanted an "A" no matter what. Please don't be like Jimmy's classmates in the 5th grade group project who don't do any of the work and still gets an "A", because Jimmy had to do twice the work. Nobody likes that kid. Don't be that adult either. Please.

Being accountable is one of the best ways to show that you

---

[35] Honestly, not trying to be harsh here. Just need to showcase the importance and gravity of this one.

BRING IN DONUTS

take pride in your work.

Be Coachable

None of us are perfect. There. I said it.

Often our most dreaded imperfections can come to light when we are working with others. And sometimes we aren't even aware of imperfections until someone brings it to our attention. That is simply no fun. When that (inevitable) day arrives, how are you prepared to handle that conversation? The day when someone might give you constructive feedback. Here's how: *Be coachable.* Here are some humbling and effective ways to be more coachable:

Be Self-Aware. Be aware of your weaknesses. Most of us know what they are by the time we get to the workplace. Don't hide them and don't have a blind spot for them. If you tend to interrupt someone, be aware of it – and work on it. If you tend to not proof-read your reports, be aware of it – and work on it.

Receive Unsolicited Feedback.

- A true collaborator can receive feedback – even if – and especially if – you haven't asked for it. This feedback can happen in the hallway and blindside you as you are jovially walking to your office. You are minding your own business and you've just been told that you are _____ (insert something that slams your ego or your intellect). Boom. More than likely, they are trying to help you or to help the project or help the organization. But even if someone is giving you the feedback as a way to make you look terrible (as a result of their insecurities[36]), be the bigger person and accept it as a way to improve yourself[37]. Please don't retaliate. Please don't be defensive. Just be receptive, even if you fundamentally don't agree with the feedback at first glance.

- If you are unclear of what they are saying, seek clarification. That will show your responsiveness to what they have said, while addressing it immediately.

- Show gratitude for the feedback, even if you don't agree with it. The giver of feedback may not remember the middle of the conversation, but they will remember how you ended it with appreciation – and simple gratitude will go a long way in your career – no matter if you are on the third day of your career or your 3,333rd[38] day of your career.

Seek Feedback.

- Genuinely and sincerely ask for constructive feedback from your colleagues. This can be from anyone. It doesn't have to be from your boss or your boss's boss. It can be from a safe person who you can trust will be honest but not brutal. It could be as simple as asking, *"What can I do to be more effective during this project?"*

- Consider the feedback a *valuable tool* in your arsenal of career development tools. It will allow you to become an even better colleague,

---

[36] I am not a psychologist. Simply a human being who has seen enough of this happen in the real world.

[37] This takes an unbelievable amount of courage and grace. It won't happen overnight. To this day, when I receive unsolicited constructive criticism I instantaneously break out into hives. Awesome.

[38] 3,333 working days is just shy of 12 years from now.

collaborator and employee. You will have an edge on all of those people who aren't as brave as you – someone who is actively looking to better themselves. It shows you are willing to make changes based on the feedback. Bravo!

Give Feedback. Once you have connected with someone and learned how to communicate with them, a way to effectively collaborate with them is to give them *helpful, constructive* feedback that will serve them as individuals. Do this with extreme caution. Check your intent for giving the feedback. Use the proper communication tools to reach out to them at the right moment and using the right types of language (avoid pronouns!). Do it with grace and good intentions. You may just help change someone's career in a caring and insightful way!

Being coachable transforms you into an incredible coach.

Lead By Example

You are a leader at work. Whether your title says it or not, *you are a leader.*

Maybe you lead a team of hundreds, or lead a process or simply lead your own workload, *you* have the power to impact your life...your workplace...the world! That's not an exaggeration.

You are a leader. Be the leader you are proud of – every single day.

Lead with kindness, not rudeness.

Lead with respect, not fear.

Lead with integrity, not retaliation.

Lead by example, not by your words.

Be the reason that people stay at your organization. Be the shining light at your workplace. Be the breath of fresh air when times are tough and people aren't collaborating. Don't tell people that you are the leader – *act like the leader.*

The ways we connect and communicate will showcase your leadership. Not your title. Not the numbers of zeros in your paycheck. It will be your actions that showcase your leadership.

All of that being said, sometimes there are people who lead in ways that are not productive, effective or ethical – not even close. Don't let that distract you or discourage you from leading by a good example. Wouldn't it be so much sweeter to succeed as a leader while being kind, gracious and professional – and to be part of the movement of making the workplace a better place! Wouldn't it be nicer to lead with a network of people that admire you for your success, not loathe you for it?

Humility check: There are entire bookshelves at bookstores on this topic. I won't pretend to be the one true expert on this topic. But I can tell you that having been led by a variety of leaders in my career, that leading by a good example does matter. It is why I have stayed at some organizations and why I have left other organizations. This is where I encourage you to read another book on this topic if you are looking for more in depth leadership insights. Those insights may change your mind in what type of leader you want to become!

People will respect a leader who leads by example and not merely by their words.

Make Your Boss's Job Easier

One of the things that is missing from every job description is the following responsibility: *Make your boss's job easier.*

Let's be clear about one quick thing. This does not mean that you have to be friends with your boss. It just means that you need to effectively collaborate with your boss in a way that makes both of you look great.

Here are some ways to make their job easier:

Communicate with them in the way they prefer. As previously mentioned, communicate with them in the way they prefer.

- When is the best time to approach them?
- Are they a morning person or an evening person?

    If your boss be-bops into work in the morning in a great mood and a smile on their face, then have meetings in the morning. If your boss drags in with dark circles under their eyes each morning, then definitely have meetings in the afternoon. This way you are setting the meeting up for success – by picking the time that is best for your boss.

- Do they prefer email or meetings to discuss items?
- Do they like for you to just pop in with questions?

Give them solutions.
- **Physical solutions.** Do they prep a certain way for a meeting?

- Do they print out information? If so, do it for them and highlight the pertinent parts of the document for them.
- **Intellectual solutions.** If there is a situation that needs to be solved, then present the problem followed by promptly presenting the proposed corresponding solutions. It is *way* easier for a boss to respond to suggestions, rather than expect them to come up with a solution on the spot. Additionally, your boss may disagree with your proposed solutions, but at least you have been able to demonstrate that you are being proactive and have a mind of your own!

Bonus Tips:

- Access their calendar. Even if you don't know the titles of the meetings, you can see their availability. Try not to bombard them with a ton of questions if they are about to jump into a meeting in a few moments.
- Don't hover outside their doorway (or anyone's doorway). It's just kind of ann*ying.
- Use every interaction as an *opportunity* for you to develop your career. Interact wisely!
- Still have your own opinions. Still be a leader.
- **Ask the most important question as you leave every interaction with your boss.** *"Is there anything else I can do to help?"* This. This question leaves your boss knowing that you are a team member and are trying to make their job easier. It will help all of you – your boss, your organization and your reputation.

Your boss can be a valuable asset in your career. Your boss can become a lifelong mentor. Treat them as an asset and as a potential mentor. You don't have to love them or even like them – but respect their role as your supervisor. They can add more value to your career than you can fathom.

Making your boss's job easier will impress your boss, showcase your professionalism, keep you on the top of their mind when new opportunities arise and strengthen this connection – for now and in the future.

Your boss can have an immense impact on your career. Interact with them wisely.

Real-Life Example

As mentioned in the real-life example for communication, it is clear that the legal department isn't always exactly the most popular crowd at some companies. The sales and marketing departments are often the cool departments at companies. Legal is near the bottom of the popularity chain in some organizations - if not the bottom.

And when you aren't the cool kid at school (or organizations), you don't often get invited to the parties (or in this case, meetings). And when you aren't invited to crucial meetings, you don't have all of the information needed to do your job and give good advice.

So, what's an unpopular colleague to do?[39]

Wait for it....I simply asked to be invited to the marketing meetings. I prefaced the invitation request by saying that I wouldn't go to these meetings as a fun sponge[40], but as an information sponge - just looking to gather insights and information without posing legal questions/gasps/eyebrow raisings.

So, I broke into the cool crowd[41] and got invited to some marketing strategy meetings. And I just absorbed the information. No legal questions.

The next part was the best part. With that additional marketing information, I was better able to *collaborate*

---

[39] In all honestly, lawyers are often the most hilarious and witty people. Many of my best friends are lawyers - and they are hands down the funniest people around the workplace. Give them a chance.

[40] You know. The people that suck all of the fun out of a situation.

[41] Not in real life. I'll never be cool. I'm about as nerdy as they come.

with my colleagues because I better understood their perspective. Thus, I was able to give quick, effective and relevant advice. (And I quite possibly went up a rung on the popularity ladder at work.)

Being proactive with your colleagues in order to better work with them is such an effective way to collaborate. Give it a whirl.

Stop being the fun sponge at work. You know, the one sucking the fun out of everything.

Have Fun

You spend too much time at the workplace not to have some fun once in a while.

Yes, this section needs to be in this book.

Yes, it is important.

Yes, it works.

Now that we got that out of the way, let's be totally honest with each other. Despite doing an AMAZING job of connecting, communicating and collaborating...work days in a cube (or in an office) can get a bit bland. Dare I say boring once in a while? Let's liven it up a bit.

Here are some easy, inexpensive ways to connect with your colleagues, improve your company culture and have some fun!!!

For some of these activities, please make sure you check with your supervisor or the HR department to make sure the activities won't disrupt the flow of business. Use your best judgment on when to involve them. The more transparent you are with them, the better reception you are likely to get from them!

Having fun at work is better than a cup of coffee. Okay, maybe not, but a close second.

Laugh Together

What's more fun that laughing with someone? Honestly, I can't think of anything much better than that.

Who would you rather work with? A company that has a jovial vibe or one that has a serious vibe all of the time? If the productivity and revenue is the same at both companies, I'm guessing that at least 94%[42] of you would pick the environment that has smiling employees.

Let your guard down a bit. Be the real you. Be transparent by showing off your most ridiculous laugh or cackle.

Share a good laugh with someone at work. And I don't mean that timid smile with a fake giggle. I mean those belly laughs that end up with someone either hyperventilating, slapping their knees or snorting. Can you please try it?

Laughing is a like a magnet. People will be drawn to you. People will enjoy spending time with you and working with you.

By laughing with your colleagues, you can single handedly change the culture of your organization in a good way. Changing the culture in a good way will help with new hires and retaining employees. Embracing happiness and laughter in the workplace is a highly desirable aspect of a company. You can bring some joy to what might be an otherwise mundane place. Remember, you are a leader, so lead with joy and cackles!

---

[42] Not a real stat. Simply an educated guess here.

Quick cautionary tales:

- It goes without saying[43] that there must be a balance in laughing and getting down to work. Please don't goof around so much that you aren't getting your work done - or are preventing others from doing their work.
- Please don't ever laugh at the expense of another person. That's just mean.
- Also, keep it clean, people. *Keep it clean.*

No matter how or who you have a laugh with, do it immediately and see how laughter can positively impact the organization!

Laugh it up at work. It will definitely improve your day.

---

[43] Okay, I'll say it anyway...

Decorate

Spice up your work space! Just like laughter, making your work space a bit more fun will make for a better work culture - for you and your colleagues.

This one has taken me some time to implement in my own career. Up until recently, I tried to compartmentalize my work life and my personal life when it came to decorating my desk. No more, my friends! I have pictures of my husband, kids and inspirational sayings on the walls. It feels a bit more like home when I walk up to my desk.

Here are some easy ways to have fun by decorating different aspects of the workplace:

Office.

- **Pictures!** We all have so many electronic pictures, but what about looking at physical pictures of your loved ones, scattered about your work space. What a great way to bring some instant joy into your day. And it's a great way to connect with someone – in case you don't have a donut on hand. People are always intrigued by the people in our pictures. Share who they are and how much you love them!
- **Inspirational Quotes.** Handwrite, print or buy some quotes that mean something to you. They will keep you going on those tough days.
- **Mousepads.** There are so many cool and fun designs for mousepads. They can really be a statement piece of an office. Find one that suits you.
- **Balloons.** Balloons are magical things. Just buy

some and put them in someone's cube or in someone's office for doing a great job. Fun. And. Magical.

- **Flowers/Plants.** Fake or real. Buy flowers or a plant for yourself. Put them in a cute (or handsome) vase. If they bring you joy, then invest in yourself and in your work space. You won't regret it.

Paperwork.

- **Funny Ink Stamps.** Why not bring some smiles to the workplace by stamping documents with a personalized or funny stamp? They have DISLIKE or LIKE stamps. Too funny. Check out a variety of other hilarious stamps that could bring some fun to the daily grind. Yes!

- **Highlighters.** If humility is the unsung hero of most people's careers, then highlighters are the unsung heroes of most people's office. They *literally* highlight the importance of certain aspects of a document. They have a variety of colors and sizes. They make the world go 'round. Make your office sing with the highlighting that happens in your office. Highlight away. Today and every day.

- **Colored Pens.** Nearly as important as highlights, colored pens can bring a real pop to anyone's documents. Find the color that you like and own it. If you like to yell, try red.

Meetings.

- **Picture wall.** Display a fun collection of pictures that showcase employees at events or employees just having a good time at the workplace. When meetings don't start right on time, it can be a great way to break the ice or reminisce about some great memories that the organization gave to its employees.

- **Legos® or Play-Doh®**[44]**.** Always have some available in your conference room. They add an element of color and encourages people to chat. Also, some people are tactile people who need something to do with their hands. It could really engage people who are typically on their phone instead during meetings. Dual purpose – fun and productivity. Win-win!

- **Puzzles.** Have a giant puzzle on a card table in the corner of the conference room. Have everyone work on it while there is down time during meetings. You could frame the completed puzzles when they are done and decorate the conference room or the lobby. How fun!

These are just a smidgen of ideas. Try one. Try them all. Decorate your workplace with some fun, my friends!

Decorate your workplace. But definitely not with glitter.

---

[44] Legos is a registered trademark of The Lego Group. Play-Doh is a registered trademark of Hasbro, Inc. This book has not been endorsed by Legos or Play-Doh.

Monthly Events

Want to bring more camaraderie to the workplace?

Want to connect with your colleagues?

Want to have some laughs at work?

Have some scheduled monthly events! They don't have to be expensive and they don't have to take up too much time. The investment is worth it to bring people together and create some enjoyable memories together as an organization.

Here are some easy ideas that go beyond the standard holiday party in December:

- **January 19th – National Popcorn Day.** Have a popcorn bar. Different seasonings and recipes. Delish!

- **February 9th – National Bagel Day AND National Pizza Day.** A-mazing. Make pizza bagels. Bang – you've celebrated two of the most important holidays in February with one culinary classic.

- **March 2nd – Dr. Seuss Day.** Start every meeting with someone reading an excerpt of their favorite Dr. Seuss book. You could even turn it into a costume day – rather than on Halloween. All of the bright colors would really impact the workplace in a fun way.

- **April 15th – Tax Day.** Everyone could wear black to signify being in the black - and not being in the red. Get it? Is that a good tax joke? If that is too lame (probably), there is always Grilled Cheese Day on April 12th.

- **May 15th – National Chocolate Chip Day.** Have a dessert bar where every dessert has chocolate chips in it. How delightful!
- **June 1st – <u>National Donut Day</u>.** *Obviously,* this should be heavily celebrated at every work place. Every single year.
- **July 1st – International Joke Day.** Have a stand-up comedy contest at lunch. Get a panel of judges or the audience can cast ballots. What a riot!
- **August 13th – National Left-Handers Day.** Make everyone write with their non-dominant hand for the day. Can you imagine all of the notepads? They would be illegible. I'm actually laughing out loud while writing this...ha ha!
- **September 26th – Johnny Appleseed Day.** Oh, the possibilities. It could be a costume contest or an apple pie contest. So fun!
- **October 31st – Halloween.** Have a pumpkin carving party. Or a gourd painting party (for those of us who are disgusted by pumpkin guts[45]).
- **November – Cyber Monday.** During lunch hour, everyone come to the conference room and find the best deals on the ol' interweb. That way people don't have to hide their shopping and collectively everyone can get better deals.
- **December 15th - National Cookie Day.** Sugar

---
[45] No joke here. My husband and I outsource our kids to anyone who will carve pumpkins with them. Every. Single. Year.

BRING IN DONUTS

cookies! Chocolate Chip Cookies! Gingerbread Cookies! Bring on the cookies. I mean, let's be honest...no one starts their diet until January anyway...

Get creative. Find some easy ways to connect the workplace by having fun at your organization. Enjoy!

Celebrate some of the obscure holidays at work. Or the yummy ones, like National Donut Day.

Activities

In addition to (or instead of) monthly scheduled events, what if you had activities at the workplace that would add an element of fun to the daily workload?

Try some of these creative ways to bring some joy to the workplace:

Potluck. Have a potluck. Maybe ask everyone to bring something that starts with a certain letter. (Let me know what letter brings the best types of food!) Ask people to leave copies of their recipes. What a great way to connect with people rather than over a stressful matter that is lingering at your computer! And it's delicious.

Lunch n' craft. Do a craft at lunch. Every season someone could host a different craft. Something easy. You could find one-gazillion ideas online! Imagine the laughs when there is that one person who struggles to follow the directions.[46]

Netflix®[47] lunch[48]. Order some pizza and get a group to watch one show a week during the lunch hour. Try some office-based sitcoms that could bring some "reel" laughs to the office.

Drawing contest. Put up chalkboard or whiteboard – and have a drawing contest. You could put the rules on the edge of the board and have a vote on it. (And let's keep this clean, people!)

---

[46] Read: me.

[47] Netflix is a registered trademark of Netflix, Inc. This book has not been endorsed by Netflix.

[48] Can you tell I think about food a lot?

BRING IN DONUTS

Scavenger Hunt. Have a scavenger hunt to ask for office supplies or company historical information. Can you imagine how fun that would be? The options are endless! There could be a small company branded prize – or the company tickets to local events – or a free 1/2 day.

Lawn games. Keep them available for people throughout the day. People could have a meeting while playing bocce ball. The fresh air combined with the fellowship is a recipe for workplace fun!

Stay active with your colleagues. Step away from your desk once in a while. Obviously, don't let the activities take away from your responsibilities. You are an adult. You know the difference. So, have fun and work hard.

Have some fun at work. Play bocce ball. Have a potluck. Eat a donut.

Start a Club

Bring like-minded people together on a regular basis to have fun at the workplace. How great! A way to boost morale? A way to meet new people in different departments? A way to do something you love? Check. Check. Check.

Here are some fun clubs you could start at work:

Baking club. Share recipes. Share techniques. Share goodies!

Movie club. Watch the movies of the books you don't have time to read. You could try themes based on what is happening in the workplace...comedy, mystery, suspense, etc. You could try to watch all of the Best Motion Picture Winners.[49] Get together once a month and talk about what movies you recommend. Or go see movies together – obviously, not during work hours, my friends.

Running club. Have at it. Not my cup of tea, but apparently, there are millions of people that find running a wonderful thing. If this is for you, start a running club that runs before work, at lunch or after work. Get those endorphins pumping!

Knitting club. At lunch hour, share your favorite patterns and techniques.

Book club. Classic! Pick some great books. Maybe do non-fiction books about how to boost your career? Or popular fiction books? Or maybe poetry? Find other book

---

[49] This is on my personal bucket list. To watch all of the winners of all of the Best Winner category. When my calendar frees up, I'll get started...

lovers in the workplace – and see what types of books would be good for the group. Discuss them every month.

Sports club. Start up a sports club. Gather a group of ~~athletes~~ colleagues who want to regularly play some games together. Hockey, golf, softball, ultimate frisbee...whatever makes your heart sing! Sweat away and connect with your new teammates.

Card/Board games club. Every Friday at lunch, play board games or card games together. The options are endless and full of fun!

How would you get one of these started? See if you can work with HR to send out a survey to see if anyone would be interested. See if your organization can sponsor a club that would benefit the morale of the workforce. Or put one of those flyers with the pull-off thingies at the bottom in the lunchroom/kitchen. Or just ask someone you think that might be interested.

Start a book club at work. Better yet, start a baking club at work. Bring on the baked goods!

Donate

To give is better than to receive. Yes....100% yes!! Be a giver.

Whether it's simply a cliché or whether it's a fact based in statistics, can we all just agree that giving to others is better than receiving? So, be a giver in the workplace. Donate time or donate items. Find a way.

Time.
- **Volunteer.** Find a local non-profit organization that could use some volunteers. Work with HR or your supervisor to donate your team's precious time to a wonderful cause. Go to a food bank. Serve your fellow neighbors in a positive way. Get to know them and connect with them. Or go to the humane society and walk the dogs. Or work with the city to find a project that can enhance the community. Get out there. Make a difference. It may even have a bigger impact on you and your organization than it will on the other people. Giving makes us better people...which makes us better neighbors...which makes us better employees...which makes your organization even better.

Stuff.
- **Food drive.** Have a food drive. Ask people to bring in non-perishables and donate them to a local food bank. At lunch, you could take a field trip to the local food bank. It is an easy way to help others, while strengthening as a team. And it simply feels amazing. You are *truly making a difference*.

BRING IN DONUTS

- **Supplies.** Work with HR or your supervisor to see if your organization can donate their older supplies. Are there computers that aren't up to the organization's standards, but would be a wonderful addition to an elementary school or a library?

- **Adopt Something.** No, not an animal from the local shelter – although you could do that as an individual! What about adopting a mile of your city – and then cleaning it up and taking pride in it. Plant beautiful flowers along the side of the road.

- **Military.** Send our troops some beloved items from home. Care packages can go a long way for people who are stationed in other parts of the country/world.

- **Money.** If the only thing your organization can do is send a check[50], that's still pretty awesome, too. It can be put to good use.

Be a giver in the workplace. Donate time or donate items. It will benefit others – and yourself in tremendous ways.

---

[50] Just make sure that the organization is thoroughly researched. You want to be giving to a legitimate non-profit.

Learn Something

Be a sponge. Soak it all in. Then soak in a bit more.

Show that you are willing and able to proactively stay ahead on the current trends and technologies that impact your role. Learning something new also shows that you are agile and flexible to change - which is crucial to every employer. Your supervisor will be thrilled to see you amplify your skills and knowledge on these important workplace topics.

Language. If your company is owned by an organization from another country, ask your supervisor if you can take language classes. While you may not become fluent, at least it shows you are trying to better communicate with the leaders of the organization. And it stretches your mind just a bit more.

Software. Do you work with one particular piece of software at work every day? If so, find out how you can learn more about how to enhance that spreadsheet or better utilize the data.[51]

Speaking. Take a public speaking class. Or learn how to prepare and present in a better way. This will not only impact your organization, but will build tons of confidence. Get out there and speak, my friends!

Process. Is there a better way to accomplish something at the workplace or within your department? Watch a webinar, perform an internet search or ask someone who is an expert. Learn more about how to be more efficient in

---

[51] Personally, I always need to learn more about using software more effectively. Basically, I'm a walking IT disaster.

the *way* you do something. Powerful stuff.

Typing. Not even kidding. If you can't type quickly, then take a class! It might save you hundreds of hours over the period of a few years. Instead of pecking and hunting for keys, learn how to type quickly. A real time saver!

Seminars. Check out the learning opportunities that are already available within your organization. They might have online training webinars or be members of organizations that have online webinars that would be low/no cost and provide you with tons of valuable information.

Tuition. Some companies offer tuition reimbursement. Check with your organization and see if that is an option for you. Remember, it isn't selfish to ask them to help pay for your tuition - they will receive the value as well!

What else do you want to learn about – that can help you with your job or help your organization? Find a way to learn more about it. And enjoy it!

Be a learning sponge. Soak it all in. Then soak in a bit more.

Real Life Example

Giving back.

One of the all-time favorite memories of my career is when our department donated time to a local charity. Annually, we would have options of where we wanted to donate our time. One year, we had the opportunity to work with an organization that gave clothing to people in need. We sorted clothes, unpacked boxes and bonded on a new level. Working side by side with colleagues, while working towards a greater was humbling and incredible. It changed us from being colleagues to friends. It changed us. It changed me.

And have fun!!!

What ideas do you have for bringing some (clean) fun to the office? I would love to hear from you!

As a company, find a non-profit group where you can donate time. It is way safer than a trust fall. And way more rewarding.

Gratitude

Showing gratitude in the workplace will truly set you apart from all of your colleagues. And it feels pretty incredible.

What are you truly grateful for? Your health? Your relationships? Your house?

Gratitude is a lost art, but the pendulum is slowing and steadily bringing gratitude back into our personal lives. And that is terrific news!

In fact, gratitude is currently quite a relevant subject matter in the personal development world. Rightfully so. There are so many ways that being grateful and showing gratitude can change your life and the lives of others.

But, what about at work? When was the last time someone said thank you at work? When was the last time *you* said thank you at work? And really meant it?

The gratitude movement hasn't percolated its way into the workplace yet. But we can change that together, my friends. We absolutely can change that fact. You see, we spend too much time at our workplace to not to implement workplace gratitude as a daily principle.

Here are some great ways you can showcase gratitude in the workplace...today!

Gratitude is a lost art. Let's bring it back!

Say Thank You

We've already discovered the importance of connecting with our colleagues...so you already remember the value of looking someone in the eyes.

Imagine the power of looking someone in the eyes...wait for it...and telling them thank you. And actually meaning it. Really meaning it.

But what on earth should I thank someone at work for? Glad you asked! Here are some things you could say thank you for in person:

Opening the door
Letting you borrow a pen
Explaining how this @%*#! printer works
Giving you a good laugh
Helping on a project
Sharing their whipped cream (as your coffee lid ... remember that awesome tip?)
Setting up a meeting
Lunch
Parking within the lines
Hiring you

It's hard *not* to think of things to say thank you for in the workplace.

Please try it. Please savor the moment of gratitude. Please spread gratitude in the workplace.

P.S. - Quick note: Just as kindness does not equal weakness, gratitude does not equal weakness either. It just doesn't.

BRING IN DONUTS

Gratitude does not equal weakness. Gratitude equals amazement.

Type Thank You

This is probably the easiest of all of the workplace gratitude tips.

Just remember the manners we learned as a kid. After someone does something to help you, *even it is just doing their job*, say thank you. Thank someone after they help answer a question on an email.

In this case, you simply type "Thank you." Two simple words that barely take any time to type. Two simple words that will set you apart from your colleagues. Two words that can help change the world.[52]

For those who might think that they couldn't possibly waste their time on typing two more words, here's a shortcut: "Thanks." One word. We all have room in our emails to add one more word.

Word of caution: There may come a time when someone asks you to stop sending them thank you emails. It's happened to me twice in my career. That's two people out of the thousands of people I have emailed in my career. Not too bad of odds. In both cases, I didn't take offense and I simply stopped sending thank you emails out of respect of their inbox. But you better believe that I thought about sending them a thank you email.

Thanks!

---

[52] No joking here, my friends. Every single time we showcase gratitude in the workplace we are slowly and steadily changing the workplace culture into a better environment for ourselves and for our future generations. We can be part of the tipping point. The point where they look back and do studies on determining when/how the workplace become a more appreciative place.

BRING IN DONUTS

Thank someone for just doing their job. It will make their day better - and your day better, too.

Write Thank You

When was the last time you received a handwritten note? At home? At work? I've received about six handwritten notes in my career - and I still have them all. They mean that much to me.

When was the last time you sent a handwritten note? Personally or professionally?

In our digital world, there is *untapped power* in the written word. Untapped power in opening an envelope of a handwritten note.

HOMEWORK (gasp!): This is the only homework in this book. Write a thank you note. Send it today. Make someone's heart beam with pride when they read your lovely note. Do it today! Today before you leave the office, write a thank you note. To anyone. It can be to someone who bought your lunch, someone who gave you advice or someone who gave you a chance. Just thank them. You may forget about writing the note, but they will never forget about how they felt when they opened that note.

The thank you note must be authentic. You must not expect anything in return. If you do, it defeats the entire purpose of the thank you note and you might as well not bother sending it to them.

So, send a thank you note to someone who took a chance on hiring you or who bought you lunch or who went above and beyond in a project.

BRING IN DONUTS

In case you are at a loss for words, here are two sample thank you letters appropriate for the workplace:

[For Boss]

Dear _____,

Just wanted to thank you so much for your ongoing support in my role at (your company). Thanks for identifying my skills and helping me to provide value to (your company). I truly appreciate all you do for our team.

My best,

_____

[For Colleague]

Dear _____,

Thank you so much for your recent help on (name of project). Your ability to collaborate and lead our team, while still bringing humor in every situation, is both appreciated and valued. Thanks again.

Sincerely,

_____

My goal is simple: To get one million thank you notes into the mail. We are a few hundred into this goal....help get us there! And let me know if you sent one. And how it was received!

Handwritten thank you notes can change the world.

Bonus: Traveling Gratitude Board.

Looking for a cool way to bring gratitude to work in a bigger, more impactful way? Try a traveling gratitude board!

Get a small chalkboard or whiteboard. Each week, keep it at someone's desk and anonymously have their colleagues write what they are grateful for about that person. Then take a picture and have it printed for that person.

What a cool reminder of what people appreciate about you!

Real Life Example

A few years into my career, I applied for a job that I had no business applying for because I didn't have the exact skill set or the amount of experience for the job. Somehow, I got an interview. Fast forward a few weeks and I eventually got the job. What in the world? How did I get this job? Three words: Thank you note.

That probably sounds far-fetched. I'm not even close to kidding about this story, though.

A few months after I got the job, I asked my boss why they picked me for the job. (I was still entirely bamboozled as to why they picked me out of all of the other candidates.) He didn't skip a beat and said I was the only person out of countless interviewees who sent a handwritten thank you note. He went on to say that while it was a nice gesture and all – even though the thank you note quickly went in the garbage – the thank you note was why I was hired because it meant that I would treat clients well. He understood that in service industries, being grateful and appreciative of your clients goes a lot farther than many other skills that people have on their resume.

Bam!

Sending personalized thank you notes can set you apart from all of the other interview candidates. And it is just the right thing to do.

Conclusion

Go find your local donut shop. This morning.

Change your career as you plop down those donuts at your workplace.

Use these sweet tips to change the trajectory of your career.... day by day.... in an ethical, effective and easy way.

Be the leader that your grandma would be proud of, as you bring professionalism and kindness back to the workplace while skyrocketing your career.

We can bring professionalism back to the workplace.

We can be kind.

We can work hard.

We can have fun.

We can be resourceful.

We can be proud of the kind of employees we are.

We can be proud of the place where we work.

It is my *genuine hope* that these practical tips are things you can implement as soon as you get back to your workplace.

It is my *genuine hope* that these empowering tips will help you make a positive impact on yourself and on your employer.

It is my *genuine hope* that these fun tips will help you change the way you work every single day.

Now go out there and navigate the workplace in an enjoyable and effective way!

I simply can't wait to hear about all of your success stories!

Grab a donut. Snag a napkin. Launch your career.

About the Author

Darcy Miller is a workplace expert, an attorney and a standup comedy dropout.

Despite being the first attorney in her entire family, she quickly rose up the corporate ladder as a result of her genuine work ethic, resourcefulness and professionalism.

While practicing law has been the foundation of Darcy's professional career, she's also been celebrated for mastering the art of facilitating understanding, collaboration and connection between just about any groups of people.

Darcy is on a mission to transform the world through kindness. By showing how kindness – to yourself and your colleagues – can be leveraged as a tool to create positive change in any workplace.

Most importantly, she is the proud mother of 3 beautiful children and she is the wife of the most supportive husband in the entire world.

Made in the USA
Monee, IL
26 January 2021